Praise for *Moonlight Rests on My Left Palm*

"Yu Xiuhua's *Moonlight Rests on My Left Palm*, translated by Fiona Sze-Lorrain, grows out of highly personal terrain. This farmer-poet says in an essay (*Moonlight* is sectioned by eight lyrical essays): 'We have manhandled so many words that I only dream of using them anew.' Yu says exactly what she means; and Sze-Lorrain honors the feeling and music in intimate translation. Thus, the poet's language rises out of the natural, tinged by elemental soil and light."

—Yusef Komunyakaa, author of *Everyday Mojo Songs of Earth*

"'Truth once spoken tends to be false,' writes Yu Xiuhua in her incredible debut of essays and poems. I am smitten with Yu's powerful writing, erotic poetry, and reflections on disability in daily life. One poem reads, 'So risky, so heavy / O this love.' I want nothing but risk in poetry and I feel proud to be a disabled poet in Yu's company."

—The Cyborg Jillian Weise, author of *Common Cyborg*

"I love reading these poems and essays by Yu Xiuhua. I feel befriended by them, by her. Courage, honesty, a love of words, and a wry sense of humor run through the pages of *Moonlight Rests on My Left Palm*, translated with grace and simplicity by Fiona Sze-Lorrain. When Yu writes in an essay, 'There is no better ode to life than a weed that grows ruthlessly and arches out of the ground, despite its trauma,' we know she is telling us her own story. And yet, in a poem called 'Wheat Has Ripened,' she says, 'I am pleased to have landed here / like a sparrow skirting through the sky-blue.' How can we be anything but grateful to a poet who ends a poem of love lost: 'I still hope / to err over and over'?"

—Mary Helen Stefaniak, author of *The Cailiffs of Baghdad, Georgia*

"I couldn't stop underlining phrases, sentences, whole passages that I wanted to quote, and think about! Yu Xiuhua's marvelous collection, a hybrid of poetry and poetical essays, each reflecting back on the other, is a transport into the soul, heart, and sensibility of a unique and exquisite mind. Fiona Sze-Lorrain's translation, generous with silence, space, and pitch-perfect transparency, is a triumph in its own right. This is the sort of book that you'll want to share immediately with your most thoughtful friend."

> —Minna Zallman Proctor, author of *Landslide: True Stories*, editor of *The Literary Review*, and translator of Natalia Ginzburg and Fleur Jaeggy

Moonlight Rests on My Left Palm

Moonlight Rests on My Left Palm

Poems
and
Essays

Yu Xiuhua

Translated from the Chinese by Fiona Sze-Lorrain

ASTRA HOUSE | NEW YORK

Astra House
A Division of Astra Publishing House
astrahouse.com

Printed in the United States of America

Publisher's Cataloging-in-Publication Data

Names: Yu, Xiuhua, 1976-, author. | Sze-Lorrain, Fiona, translator.
Title: Moonlight rests on my left palm : poems and essays / Yu Xiuhua ; translated from the Chinese by Fiona Sze-Lorrain.
Description: New York, NY: Astra House, 2021.
Identifiers: LCCN: 2021909547 | ISBN: 9781662600470 (hardcover) | ISBN: 9781662600487 (ebook)
Subjects: LCSH Chinese poetry—Translations into English. | Chinese poetry—21st century—Translations into English. | Chinese poetry—Women authors. | Nature—Poetry | BISAC POETRY / Asian / Chinese | POETRY / Women Authors | POETRY / Subjects & Themes / Nature
Classification: LCC PL2973.X58127 M66 2021 | DDC 895.11—dc23

First edition

10 9 8 7 6 5 4 3 2 1

Design by Richard Oriolo
The text is set in Optima LT Std.
The titles are set in SangBleu OG Sans.

Contents

Translator's Note

WHEN I BEGAN TO TRANSLATE Yu Xiuhua, I had, to my embarrassment, only read one of her poems, "Crossing Half of China to Fuck You." Widely known as Yu's most "notorious" poem, it was posted online in October 2014 and went viral. With its catchy title and raw language, the piece speaks explicitly about sex and the poet's craving for it:

> I penetrate a hail of bullets to fuck you
> I press countless dark nights into one dawn to fuck you
> I, as many, run as one to fuck you

Given the patriarchal and Confucianist influences that dominate contemporary Chinese society, it is rare for a "foreigner" like me to come across a Chinese woman poet not yet forty writing about sex so openly—and "desperately"—let alone a farmer with cerebral palsy who is completely self-taught. Yu Xiuhua's life and work has been mediatized nationwide, however. Reception in the male-dominated world of Chinese poetry has been mixed: some interpret the poet's longing for love as plain "lust," some feel offended by Yu's "unrefined" language (she is a high school dropout) and are embarrassed by what they read, some show compassion for her difficult life and admire her courage, and others affirm the therapeutic and spiritual force of poetry, whereas others yet express their enthusiasm for this new confessional voice in the Chinese literary mainstream.

Yu Xiuhua suffers from cerebral palsy, and until she reached celebrity status as a best-selling poet, she lived a life of poverty in a rural village of Hubei Province, trapped in a deeply unhappy arranged marriage: this much I knew when I first discovered her work in 2014. However, I knew close to nothing about her grueling life and outbursts of creativity. Neither had I watched the feature documentary *Still Tomorrow* (2016), directed by Jian Fan, that brought Yu Xiuhua's womanhood, farm life, poetic work, and ongoing struggles to the screen. During the early months of translating Yu's work, I read her poems aloud and let them speak first and directly to me. As her translator, I have learned how her life and disability have shaped her poetry in a unique voice that must be heard just as it is. I have chosen beauty and austerity by seeking to translate Yu Xiuhua simply, quietly, paying attention to every nuance of her work. I, for one, want to listen to what Yu Xiuhua wants to tell us. When she reads her poems aloud, she sometimes stammers or painfully contorts her body and twists her face before a word can be muffled or pronounced. As much as we can never exactly relate to the body and suffering she lives in, we each have the capacity to listen harder to what she would like to share. To render these English versions in a more authentic voice, I aim not to aestheticize her idiosyncratic syntax but to generate, through silence, possibilities for readers to hear better in each piece what Denise Levertov has called the "inner voice," the one a poet hears when "constantly talking to himself, inside of himself, constantly approximating and evaluating and trying to grasp his experience in words."[1]

In these selected poems and essays, I have discovered a courageous woman not lacking emotional contradictions, hunger, and naivety. Her drive for a more meaningful life, propelled by a passion for poetry, found a contagious mass appeal in her country. Thanks to the Internet, Yu discovered a way to connect with the outside world and share her poetry. But how did Yu find poetry—or rather, how did poetry and the muses find her? This remains a mystery, probably even for the poet herself: after all, it is poets themselves

---

[1] Denise Levertov, "Line-breaks, Stanza-spaces, and the Inner Voice," *The Poet in the World* (New York: New Directions, 1973), 24.

who know best how unfathomable the source and how inex-
plicable the beginnings of their poems can be. Having
divorced her estranged husband in recent years—despite her
physical vulnerability, humble background, and the stigma of
being a divorcée and single mother in a poor, marginal, tradi-
tional Chinese village—Yu Xiuhua is in no way less feminist
or modern than her Chinese contemporaries. But in her
poems she strikes me as more feminine than feminist—by
feminine, I am thinking of a fellow poet-translator, Johannes
Göransson's comment on the South Korean woman poet
Kim Hyesoon's "sense of the feminine": "the feminine is a
state of receptivity, defined by inclusiveness. The feminine
becomes a site where all voices are heard."[2] Contrary to
what some "elite" critics and poets in China have pointed
out, Yu Xiuhua's all-embracing yearning for tenderness and
love—physical, romantic, or spiritual—seems much less ide-
ological or propagandist than humane and concrete. In the
poem "I Love You," for example, she states matter-of-factly:

> In my dumb life, I draw water from a well, cook, take
>   my medicine regularly
> When the sun is fine, I place myself inside it, like a dried
>   orange peel
> Tea leaves to use on alternate rounds: chrysanthemum,
>   jasmine, rose, lemon

---

[2] Johannes Göransson, "Grotesque Poems, Haunted Translations: The Blackened
Space of Kim Hyesoon and Don Mee Choi," *Transgressive Circulation: Essays on
Translation* (Blacksburg: Noemi Press, 2018), 75.

In another, titled simply "Love," she evokes the tranquil countryside of her Hengdian Village, and reveals how this rural environment shapes her unique sense of inclusiveness within a vaster universe, while hinting at a clandestine, unrequited passion:

I will run into the best landscape, the best folk
Wherever they are is my homeland
an ancestral temple where I hear stars in dialogue

Here I am, at this hour
The world shows me how landscapes undulate
However large its secret, however large the sky it opens

At this instant, struck by a secret
I weep, but keep my mouth shut

Writing love poems is a challenge, as most—if not all—poets know. How does one express the immortal love without banalizing or abusing the word itself? Yu Xiuhua's love poems aren't just for her lover and herself; they are for the world at large: nature, animals, objects, words, and beauty. In poetry and prose, Yu Xiuhua uses the word *love* freely and without disguise, and seems unafraid of sentimentalizing its specific contexts or implied connotations. For instance, Zhang Simon, a journalist for the online *ABILITY Magazine* notes that the word *love* appears more than a hundred and forty times in Yu's poetry published in 2014 and 2015.[3] As I translate, I realize how at once translatable and untranslatable "love" is, noun or verb. It is a constant variable that, to some degree, puts a check on interpretation and renders it pointless. For Yu Xiuhua, love is more a complex than a reality or a fact that materializes. One of my colleagues, the scholar Dian Li, wrote an essay that makes mention of Yu Xiuhua's response to a television host regarding her interest "in the subject of love": "The less I have, the more I want to write about it." Li adds, "The host then went on to wish her good luck in finding her true love soon . . . but Yu Xiuhua's answer, 'Maybe in my next life,' stunned the host and the live audience."[4]

The less I have, the more I want to write about it. How eloquent. I only wish I could say this as well as Yu Xiuhua, but in another language and culture.

FIONA SZE-LORRAIN

---

[3] Simon Zhang, "Poetic Documentation—Yu Xiuhua," *ABILITY Magazine,* Issue 142, abilitymagazine.com/poetic-documentation-yu-xiuhua/.
[4] Dian Li, "Yu Xiuhua: A Life Lived in Poetry," *World Literature Today* 92, no. 4 (July–August 2018): 28.

Moonlight Rests on My Left Palm

Crossing Half of China to Fuck You

Fucking you and being fucked by you are quite the same, no more
than the force of two colliding bodies, a flower coaxed into blossom
No more than a flower, a fictional spring we mistake for a renewed life
Half across China, anything can happen: volcanoes erupt, rivers parch
some neglected political prisoners and refugees
an elaphure and a Manchurian crane at gunpoint
I penetrate a hail of bullets to fuck you
I press countless dark nights into one dawn to fuck you
I, as many, run as one to fuck you
Of course butterflies can lead me astray
and I think of some odes as spring

My Crazy Love Feels More Like Despair[5]

ONE CAN'T HELP BUT FEEL brazen and impudent at the thought of analyzing a poem after having written it. Thankfully, I am used to being brazen and impudent. My fragile soul—if I have one—is no longer wounded by such humiliation. Nowadays, I seem more willing to talk about the *soul*, a nothingness, an absence or a presence. Poets have mixed feelings about this word, as it is as much misused as *love*.

---

[5] The original essay begins with the poem "Crossing Half of China to Fuck You," in a version that contains three additional verses at the end: "think of a village like Hengdian as my hometown // These / are the key reasons why I fuck you."

On yet another quiet night, rain pitter-patters in the courtyard. A profound, vast darkness hangs between raindrops. Because of the rain, it feels like even more of an abyss. After an interminable period of solitude, like someone who no longer knows if she is dead or alive, I can't tell if my room, still brightly lit, is an impenetrable refuge or the sparks of a firefly in the dark. Yet my heart burns so ardently for this instant. On my computer I create a document, and bliss comes to me as words leap onscreen one by one.

At last I understand that bliss is both concrete and attainable. One does not lose sight of bliss as easily as one may imagine. I am grateful for the strength to find this bliss.

All along, I have claimed to be a woman without a story. Still, I seem to have experienced much of life. How deplorable I am—one of those women who creates her own plot, speciously and without details. Unable to pull ourselves out of our miserable loneliness, we even get enraged when someone dares break our illusion.

While my poetry received substantial media attention, some began to look into the narrative in my poetry: a woman writer had been publishing online stories about her travels. These were well-written accounts that garnered high praise. Soon, a critic pointed out factual inaccuracies in the stories, in spite of the "beautiful language." The writer denied the inaccuracies vehemently, insisting that the tourist attraction was exactly as she had depicted it. Debates were followed by violent verbal attacks against her. What was originally a felicitous event turned into something melodramatic and absurd.

Later, an insider leaked the news that the writer was in fact a disabled person who couldn't possibly have traveled to all these places. She had cooked up stories based on materials she found online. However wild an imagination, it would never be perfect; a loophole soon surfaced. I don't know what her mistake was in the first place, given the consequences. More disastrously, she persisted in her denial, and argued with those familiar with those sites. I can't understand how an ego can be so unyielding, even in moments of confusion when it can't discern the real from the imagined.

This incident has lingered in my mind for several days, as I recall past quarrels with others online, and how I insisted that nothing was ever invented or not factual. To some extent, I am a realist. I am not fond of fiction, but can understand this woman then: stuck in one place, she desperately longed to go out and see the world, so she invented different "selves," deceiving her own heart while it yearned for freedom. How my heart aches for her, albeit reluctantly. How complex this heartache would be, had this fictitious world contained more artifice.

The rain has stopped indistinctly, as it still casually strikes down somewhere. The night seems to lighten up. Of course, this is no more than an illusion created by sounds: the hour is late, like a disease that spreads in one's life. Night settles atop our heads. Rather than being suspended in midair, it falls heavily in times of need, crushing us into the mud, emptying the dusty, mortal world.

I am at a loss, but rightly so: I think I can live a painless life without love, even though this isn't exactly truth beyond doubt. Until now, I have loathed myself for not being more promiscuous, or not continuing to be promiscuous. I am in a dilemma about my earthly desires: I don't know how to resolve these problems properly, for this unfair life has too often made me feel ashamed of myself.

I desperately longed for love, or some proof of my own existence. There are enough reasons for my existence, but without love, I am doubtful. Thinking back, I must have been pitting myself against my own self: the world has fulfilled its promise to me by allowing me to live in it, so why can't I stop my doubts and stop torturing my body into "proving the proof" of my existence?

Perhaps in the shackles of marriage, my rebellious self was in pain. I yearned for love, someone who could drag me out of my doubts. In other words, I wanted an imaginary world to break through the preexisting imagined world. I wanted to suffer to death. I wanted to destroy and be doomed forever. Fate had lowered me into a boundless swamp, and my resistance was no more than a joke in God's eyes that had to happen nonetheless.

Now, I recall how, one quiet night, I shelved my determination to "cross half of China to fuck someone." I loathe myself for having lost my determination so swiftly. I loathe that my soul, like moonlight, has yet to be invaded.

I have invented a lover in a faraway place. I hardly think of him, until one day when I inform him of my visit. He is thrilled. Tall and bearded, he is usually clean-shaven. When he shakes my hand, his large palm will painfully squeeze mine. He does not like hugs, but upon seeing me, worn out by the journey, he puts his arms around my shoulders and loves me dearly.

But more crucially, he must be a charismatic man whom I can love unconditionally, and desperately give a body I can't bear to see aging. Even though I am aware that a fusion of bodies can neither prove nor intensify love, I am now helplessly in love. Only by being in this state can I prove to myself that *I love you without reserve, not just to move your heart, since your solitude means nothing to me, but to praise your lovely existence in this world.*

Love is frivolous regardless of who we love, and before it, we humans are even smaller. The inadequacy of our being drives me to despair, which shapes my candor. Yes, I can visit you thousands of times, gracefully and quietly be your lover, but fate is ever-evolving: I fear its measured kindness, that I would be lost midway, in turn loathing my body if it failed to give you something.

Whenever I fall in love in this way, I have no idea of the wrong I have done, which is none other than the search for a path in beauty. I know I have yet to find this path, and realize that I am in fact scared of finding it. This lack of confidence is an empty self-defense. But one is never content with endless protection, let alone self-protection. I must find a quick and accessible way to breathe in this bubble.

In a daze, I once fooled around by loving two or more poets at the same time. Although I was probably more attracted to women poets, I was unaware of it until now. Often, we played around, while I never stopped feeling guilty for having led astray my adorable friends: whenever they spoke with elegance, I would ruin their eloquence with a sentence like *Fuck you!* When I was in a terrible mood, I would even say things like *Fuck your mother.*

I, too, fell in love with a poet who was in turn seduced by a lovely young woman poet. (Even now, I can't verify the truth behind this, nor can I confirm my love for him. Sadly, I have realized that men whom I love tend to be as common as muck; even more tragically, I also realize that I can't break this curse.) I didn't know who to blame, so I ended up hating myself for my ugliness and disability. Because of this vicious cycle of self-hatred, I have been walking in this world with deep sorrow: if not even an "average" man can love me, what kind of failure am I?

Along came another poet. I joked, "See, how dearly I love you. Even when people ask me who I want to fuck, I've said nothing about you." Come to think of it now, I must have let him down by not giving him a chance to be as famous as I am. I have my reasons: I do not mean what I have said in the literal sense, even though our relationship stabilized and has become valuable—I am now his distant sister, he is my kin. We have never met, and never want to.

Let me say this: by the time I truly believed in him, my poem had become wildly popular, but really, it had nothing to do with anyone—not even me. I am so disappointed. How I wish for someone whom I could fuck boldly and selflessly.

Ah Le, Again I Think of You, Alas[6]

I am afraid to give you my heart
afraid you might suffer once I think of you
I can't give you my eyes
afraid you might shed tears once I cry
I can't give you my life
Once I die, you too will disappear

I want the position behind you
When I see you, you can't see me
I want your night shadow
When I call you, you can't hear me
I want your twilight years
and make wine from now on

---

[6] Ah Le is Yu's unrequited lover.

Snow Dream

I dream of eight thousand miles of snow: from your province
    to mine, from my embroidered cloth
to your inn
this white bluff and bluster
A discarded mine buried deep, a dark river sinks into oblivion
Horse bones rise in a wild grassland
The sky, a vast hollow
You subdue whiteness in your body with three bowls of liquor
Weary of chaotic worldly affairs, you stick a pen into years of feuds
and walk south
I now have doppelgängers: one watches you float in a dream
one floats with you in a dream within a dream
Another presses down the drift patiently

To Lei Pingyang

I salute you as a poet, shake your hands as a farmer
In those days, poor and homeless, I withstood an innocent life, bought
　　a jar of wine
and invited you along
only and only because in your mind a dog barked at the autumn wind
only and only because of your solitude, confrontation, reconciliation,
　　coveting
only and only because an old poet had left, so you knelt for a long
　　time before a Buddha statue in a foreign land, choked with tears

All these years, when people ask where I am in life
I reply, *Surviving. Like you, I've never written any poetry*
In this lifetime, we meet others who write poetry, even though they aren't
　　poets to me
But you are—
coldly watching a dog die you are
calmly facing the setting sun you are
weeping through poetry for a soul who can't return, you are

and so what?
You continue to show compassion, traveling west
All I do after saluting you is to go back to my own work
Still, I want to salute you again, if only for someone who lets me cry
whose heart blossoms like a lotus
who's willing to put his heart and soul into it, and confess in blood

Those Secrets Suddenly Dignified

Your birthday, my lover, is like an apple's secret
On this unique day, you open autumn wind, appease waves
My narrative interrupted over and over, words dried up, tears
    blind and imprecise

I hand my destiny over to the night wind and you
Days are long, I become whiny when I talk about despair
O, you've given me the slenderest wings
Let me fly like a bee—how exhausting—or die en route
with a sweet stomach

I imagine the candles you light, but ask that you omit my imagination
I'm far, far behind at the scene
I see the excessive sun in Hengdian Village, chrysanthemums on a wound
I'm ashamed of them out of politeness

Forgive me for pausing again for no reason. You aren't surprised
so blow out the candles in one breath
Once I add a word, my sorrow, despair, and fury turn into beauty
This day sways, suddenly dignified

Our Whereabouts Unknown
in This Night

1

How wonderful, like plucking *qin*[7] strings deep in a mountain
Only rocks and withered leaves are audible. Water, ill
at ease
Later, even humans look cheerless; they don't shower or say good night
but sleep in melancholia

Moonshine or not, an abyss widens
I say in a pond of time, as we descend we must bear
some fears
I say indeed, this has nothing to do with *already*, or *yet*
to come

Night falls time and again. Rid of fatigue
we curl up, regardless of our collision
Ah Le, this is different from a hugging posture: what we share
is a touch of voluntary emotion
We have never said good night

---

[7] A *qin* or *guqin* is an ancient Chinese zither that contains seven strings.

2

If I calm down, I'll end up in shackles, a tug-of-war with time
When I'm not hungry, life seems uphill
If I don't eat dinner, I'll lie on the floor
let night drag me around
like a dog that can't bark

The end is the same, joy or sorrow
Oh, how different it can be for those
who go elsewhere on a train
memorize lines from nowhere
A word becomes a prophecy by mistake

You, an actor in a small city, an emcee
stuck like mud fish by the River Han
Being stuck is to make the best out of a situation
One mustn't take in all the underworld anger
Look at a city's gaze

3

Turbulence and life won't wash away
my yearning
Ah Le, both of us are sinning
I'm lit by our village plants
You are expelled by the city's neon lights

Afraid of vanishing, we hug our black caskets
Even in death, we exist in our own

veins
I've lost patience
for my zeal and your indifference

To live or not to live is one thing
but we know we have survived many years
How unforgivable
Go ahead and cough, cough
but don't cough out phlegm

4

Sigh, I can't get rid of my mysophobia
A man who can't stand love picks his nose and spits before me
When a peasant's corpse is dug out
I can't stop vomiting
can't help wanting to touch it

Death can't stop surging on, so I float
Of course I won't catch you, Ah Le
You exist not for me to catch you
but for me to pick up a knife so I know
how to reject unwanted parts

Forget it
Anyone can grow lighter, you above all
I'm speechless at this point
You sleep, I sit
Eight thousand miles of spring

I Love You

In my dumb life, I draw water from a well, cook, take my medicine regularly
When the sun is fine, I place myself inside it, like a dried orange peel
Tea leaves to use on alternate rounds: chrysanthemum, jasmine, rose, lemon
These marvels lead me to spring
Time and again I must curb snow in my heart
Too pure and close to spring

I read your poetry in a clean courtyard: these worldly things
sparrows dart past in a trance
Time is bright and clear. Melancholia isn't advisable
If you send me a book, I won't send you poetry
I want to give you a book about plants, about crops
share with you the difference between rice and weeds

share with you the spring of a weed
on tenterhooks

My Body Too Contains a Train

But I never show off. This has nothing to do with secrets
Even a hundred full moons won't move me. I stifle
the moon whistles
but someone boards the train, another alights, someone throws
    a fruit peel
and napkin out the window. Someone says this is because of spring

It doesn't plan to stop, but passes
A small plain where dew stares in a breeze
Low thatched hut, swaying chimney smoke
A boy bows his head low, sits against the light, tears undried
A flower in his hand stares
back

Mottled paint in the train in my body
It doesn't panic, but accepts drunkards, beggars, street
    performers, or any leader
Up and down
the train in my body never takes a wrong track
It embraces heavy snowfall, storm, mudslide, absurdity

A Man Stops by My Room

Two cigarette butts on the floor, their smell not dissipated
Like the way he sat on a tall wooden bench
cross-legged
watching a martial arts contest absentmindedly

I sat at the door, watched clouds, and read
observing the back of his head
how his hair grew dense by decades, enough to hide a witch
I observed the back of his head, read, watched clouds

I saw Don Quixote enter barren hills
He wrote a letter for Sancho to give to Dulcinea
then took off his clothes
and hit a rock

After the martial arts contest, he got up and said goodbye
Two cigarettes half-used but thrown away
I couldn't help
but feel disheartened

How Can I Make You Love Me

How can I make you love me as I slowly age
Morning glories, blue on a fence
sadly bluer than the sky

How can I make you love me at a lonelier hour
Millet harvested in the village, weeds dense but wilted
How can you find the way
in a starry sky

I have the heart of a virgin
full of passion for this mortal world, compassion for hatred
But in this lonely Hengdian Village
this feels like adultery
It's no secret, but no one speaks of it

Who knows what comes next after being loved, but I wait in patience
Once, I followed a glow from the beginning to the end
Despair won't linger long in the body
Even a strand of weed sways on my body
I think
this is a marvel

My Nostalgia
Differs from Yours

I HAVE A HOME, BUT no hometown. For a time, this worried me more than those who were homesick. A hometown is what you call your old home, the place where you were born and bred, where you return after having been gone. Since I have never left my Hengdian Village, I can't call it my hometown. Despite my poetic nostalgia, I sense a void in my life, as my physical limitations deprive me of the experience of having a hometown and the possibility to leave. I understand that this is but a flaw in my physical ability, just as I can't turn around a corner in my destiny. Nostalgia can move others' hearts; Yu Guangzhong's poem "Nostalgia," for instance, has been a source of inspiration to several generations. Of course, old Mr. Yu's nostalgia has become representative and national. One's nostalgia, once associated with one's country, will assume the form of the public sentiments of a people. It isn't possible, however, to generate such public feelings, as our feelings can't transcend the village.

Over time, I ceased to have grievances about not being able to leave my hometown: in the past, I channeled resentment and resistance to my own self, so much so that I did not even realize how my body and weak character had limited my means. I wasn't courageous, and life did not oppress me enough for me to turn my back against my birthplace, either. My parents kept me close under their wings and sheltered me with affection. Later, it became my child's turn to protect me. I hope my child grows up slowly. As I witness how so many children, neglected by their parents, become tormented by their solitude, I hope my child will not be affected by the uncertainties in life. All children are born independent. Walking out on our village would do more harm than good if it made my child homesick. Given these and other reasons, I stay rooted in Hengdian, where my roots grow firm as ever.

Some years ago, I was contemplating a life in quiet and peace. In the long river of life, many of us are destined to be forgotten in our minor roles. As long as one finds happiness in one's own role, one is victorious. Although I have known little happiness, I can't help but wonder: How can so many joys in life possibly exist? I feel at peace with myself, and have no further expectations of life. This seems best for me. Life is like a play. Take a closer look around: everyone is performing his or her role too seriously. I think of how we used to play poker when we were young: no money, but we were so studious, we racked our brains and analyzed each move earnestly. Destiny fears being seen through, and even being partially seen through seems irksome enough. I guess I have only partially seen through nostalgia. I observe how so many hope to return to their roots one day, and how they go around in their lives only to return to their origins. Had I left Hengdian, I know I wouldn't be spared this same fate. This is why I now live in advance of the days I would have otherwise liked to spend in the outside world.

Since I have spent my entire life on this thin leaf of Hengdian, I have never thought of being homesick, not one day. Our small village consists of more than three hundred families. So many last names—each family with its own government, existing in a somewhat identical life. In these somewhat identical times, the gap between our lives and experiences becomes so insignificant that similar times generate similar lives and people: without jealousy or hatred, only peace and contentment. In spite of poverty, one's peace and contentment is probably the balance one finds in one's way of life. This universal quest for peace and contentment fits our Chinese village culture.

Lately, or to be more precise, just two, three years ago, whenever one walked into a farmhouse, the first thing one saw was red peppers and corn hanging from the eaves. There were also some rusty iron plows under the eaves. After spring, the plows attacked the soil, their rust cleaned by the grinding so that they glowed in white heat. Every now and then, certain things in the country looked "surreal," as if in a state of waiting: *Wait until your season arrives, wait for an inner voice to open yourself up.* In fact, the entire countryside was also in a surreal state, neither in deep sleep nor wakefulness, but with eyes shut. It was the thorough transformation of our world in four seasons, one in which traces were left while passing through life. Hengdian is a relatively large natural village with over two thousand people in three hundred households. On its gently sloping, hilly terrain, several families either cohabitate or live independently of one another. Mostly, they lead quiet lives, each busy with their own affairs. Morning birds in the bamboo forest behind our houses are noisier than us humans. Magpies and doves move around in flocks, as do the sparrows. I vividly recall an afternoon when the neighborhood was under construction, several magpies flew and landed on an aspen in front of my house, bending its branches.

But Hengdian isn't a wealthy village: although it contains ample land, good policies were only implemented recently. Before, people could barely afford their exorbitant agricultural taxes. They had almost nothing left after paying those agricultural taxes. If a family yielded less than expected from its arable land, it would not make ends meet. But my honest country kin never thought of this as something unreasonable. They considered not being able to pay their taxes a disgrace; after all, my parents have been obediently doing so every year. When my brother and I were in school, they would earn extra in their spare time by collecting eggs in the village to sell in Jingmen City. They could earn five cents per egg. Their earnings from ten eggs are now nothing but spare change in a supermarket. Still, at that time, my parents earned their five cents with immense joy. They accumulated daily wealth cent by cent. To this day, I can't say how much it will cost to accumulate the wealth in my heart: a nonrequired sense of self-contentment and joy in life. People in those days had no worries, save for idle thoughts and hopes that couldn't come true. Did the idea of a marvelous life have anything to do with not having any hope? Hope was but warmth from one's heart.

Gradually, a few two-story houses emerged in our village: they were built by those who made money after leaving the village. Most went into the tofu business. Shipai is famous for its tofu, with tofu businesses everywhere. But most of its businessmen are locals residing in nearby villages. Although our village is just twenty kilometers away from Shipai, and considered one of "its" villages, far fewer of us went into tofu. It is painful for us to abandon our abundant land. Of course, it has to do with the fact that the idea of "making money" isn't yet in vogue, even though others have had success with it. It wasn't until later, when one of ours finally left Hengdian, that he was followed by others. But still, they were not many. Most of us have stayed to guard our land. This is the case for our family. There are places one can't let go, and we have reasons not to. Occasionally, someone in our family thinks about getting rich, while our parents continue to cultivate nearly twenty *mu* of land. Year after year, time is an excellent lobbyist who dissuades us from leaving, so we stay to look after our lands here and there. When the tofu men return to build their villas in the village, we are envious, of course, but since they aren't many, and we get to see these villas from afar every day, our envy soon disappears.

Over the span of twenty years, our village has seen major changes, such as the demolition of mud-wall houses. Richer families have built little villas, the poorer ones *sihe*[8] compounds and houses with tiles. When one has less money, one builds a smaller place. No one competes about houses anyway, nor does anyone feel inferior because of one's house. Such is the mentality of us Hengdian locals. A culture and civilization is based on a collective mentality. However, *culture* and *civilization* are broad terms that can't apply generically to Hengdian; one needs to take into account their specific contexts. Just as a person gets through life and misery, culture and civilization exist through hardship and time. It doesn't seem kind to exploit a precious place within a brief span. I don't know if the undulating and hilly landscape of Hengdian has contributed to the happiness of its people, or

---

[8] A *siheyuan*—literally translated as a "courtyard enclosed by buildings on four sides"—is a historical Chinese residence, one of the unique architectural traditions in China.

its people give up their pursuit of a better life once they find enough to get by. Needless to say, we don't exactly know what constitutes "a better life," nor do we know its standards. Without a criterion, anyone can come up with one. How wonderful: anyone is entitled to his or her own standards, and needs not care for others', just as everyone can be entitled to his or her own government, and exercise his or her own power. This sounds like Lu Xun's fictional character, Kong Yiji, who naively thinks his life is the best.

Gradually, Hengdian embraced the cycle of spring, summer, autumn, and winter. Some die, some are born, some leave Hengdian, others arrive. There is no ancestral hall or temple in Hengdian. The village seems abandoned by the gods, yet the gods never cease to live in the people's hearts: they know morality and do not provoke conflicts. I have been living here for forty years, and all this time no evil has ever occurred. Of course, a petty theft might take place from time to time, or a thief or a hooker might chance by. Like our human nature, my village isn't without its imperfections. I have no desire to cleanse my birthplace of them, just as we humans can't always defend humanity. Behavioral and moral blemishes often remind us to stay alert to life, to be more vigiliant of ourselves than of others, even if we never care to think of this while time goes by east and west of the sun.

By the time I reach the age of forty, my parents are over sixty. We have imagined Hengdian Village to be eternal in our lives, ready to obey and trust fate completely. Our absolute trust comes from our life experience: a time for birth and a time for death. Isn't this already a privilege? We have created poetic grace in times of poverty, in return for the earth's embrace of our bodies and souls. When we look up in between our tasks, we realize the closest existence to our village isn't the next one, but the patch of sky above us. A clear sky is a consolation and an encouragement, as well as a delusion. Once, I said to my father, "How blessed to be buried in this sky after we die." My father looked up and squinted; light from the sky had fallen into his eyes, producing fine sparkling sounds.

"No," he said, "I don't want to be buried in the sky. It isn't practical. Remember this: I must be buried in the earth." My father looked at me and added, "In any case, you can only bury me below." Then he returned to his task with a peaceful mind. But I was not convinced: no matter what, I would bury myself, or at least my soul, in the sky. My father dismissed any discussion about the soul as the most idle activity, and would not stop for such idleness. In his words, *We can't do anything about our souls, as the soul takes care of itself.* But I feel I should place myself in this sky, whether shattered or exalted, and contribute a part of myself to it. As I think of this, a sense of pride arises—my pride for Hengdian Village—and a tinge of melancholia. Thoughts coming to me in my birthplace are perhaps part of some nostalgia, but my nostalgia is "vertical," unlike "horizontal" homesickness, which is closer to emotions, the sentiments of an individual for a community. "Vertical" nostalgia feels closer to the heart, one's sentiments for another, and of course the sky. I feel a little ashamed of my self-imposed homesickness, even though my shame feels bittersweet: I am rooted to this place, but for a time did not know where my roots would grow. Now I know, like an excited girl who seems to have caught a glimpse of her own back at last.

Not only is the region under the administration of Hengdian thus considered Hengdian, the sky above is, too, Hengdian. Still, this discovery hardly brings us any joy: it is a truth that has existed all this time, but we now look up to see it anew. What seems certain is that the region of Hengdian can never change. But what about the sky above? Is it always that same sky? No doubt it has always existed, though we are just looking up to see it anew. As a region, Hengdian will never change, but is the sky above it always the same sky? This is another tricky issue. I don't know why I am so fussy about the sky as sky. I can't explain myself. We try to see the secret of the sky from our mortal world, but this is obviously an impossible task.

We love the sky above us in part because of the earth under this sky, how its spirit is reflected in the local sky. We believe so firmly in this earth because it is closely linked to our days, like life and death. The sky responds to the earth, and vice versa: even if they may not speak to each other the way life and death do, they relate to their cultures. Life and death, once endowed with a cultural heritage, find their base strength and stand strong and bold. We do not survive just on a surface world, but within a space, a three-dimensional space that our eyes can't reach but where spirits and gods live. Country ghosts and gods are simple spirits, and more likely to live in harmony with people. I often feel the choice of one's living conditions has to do with one's DNA. Take my family, for instance: right from our birth, we show little interest in flamboyance and prosperity. If anything, we merely hope for better days to get by. In our younger days, we can't see things lucidly, and blame God for not giving us a better life. We fail to understand life, and have every reason for our doubts; because of these doubts, we continue to seek out our souls and meditate, and as a result, we come to the conclusion that one's life results from the choices determined by one's DNA.

When thought bears fruits, action becomes concrete and practical: I will spend my days peacefully in this village, and peacefully accept the sun and wind in our region. God takes care of all other similar forms of life. Rather than being thinkers in life, country people act upon life directly, as action is the essence of life. If a farmer merely thinks about life instead of solving its problems, thought will soon lose its value. In other words, the value of something manifests itself differently via different individuals. A rural dweller's values in life are influenced directly by his perspectives and necessities in life. Had my countrymen known that on this splendid morning, I am writing about "value" and "worthlessness" in my new living room, they would think I had lost my mind. The value of life lies in its dribs and drabs, but my kin and folk never think of recording these in words.

Yes, I am typing these in our new living room. On New Year's Day in 2017, we moved into a new house, together with the rest of the three hundred families in our village of Hengdian. Households originally scattered in all corners across a few thousand *mu* are now in a cluster. Now that we live at close quarters, whenever one raises one's voice at home, one can be heard by a few families down the road. This is none other than the new socialist village! Years ago, when Hengdian made plans for its new countryside, the villagers were delighted. They could now buy a decent house at a reasonable price, which was never accessible for some in their lifetime anyway. Since the plan was to build a "new village" near where we lived, our lands were quickly requisitioned. My parents and I were reduced from being "landlords" of nearly twenty *mu* to landless people. But my parents are getting on in years, and finding it increasingly tough to work in the fields, so having our lands requisitioned at that time wasn't a bad thing after all; at least it would put an end to their labor, and compel them to relax in old age and retirement. But this was not the case for everyone: not every piece of land was requisitioned, nor everyone soon to retire. Had our lands not been requisitioned, my parents would have needed to work into their eighties and until their last breath. Labor has brought us enough grief and sorrow, and grievances. I don't see it as an ode to life. The "exquisite bridges and flowing water" one finds in poetry are not written by real farmers, but those who claim to love rural life when they most fear it. Secretly, I rejoice that my parents no longer have to do farm work, but can't help but worry: How can we now provide for our own needs? This is truly an alarming concern, as fundamentally we no longer eat what we grow, so we no longer live with a peace of mind. I don't mean to say that we feel ill at ease with food grown by others, but such a change in our lifestyle has apparently shattered the surety of a tradition: even though progress suggests civilization, a civilization and culture arises because of its priceless traditional customs.

A new village is thus born on the land of Hengdian, albeit a little abruptly. Had someone left home for work after a year, he wouldn't be able to find his home when he came back for the New Year. But for the most part, people seem happy with their renovated houses, which appear no different from the ones in the city. Perhaps they, too, live more comfortably: water facilities, heating, green projects, and excellent community services. What we used to see on TV has now come alive, right here, and even better, in our very own village of Hengdian. Those who live far away can now travel easily to see us: geographical distance between us humans is now cut back. I don't know if we villagers, too, hope to cut back our psychological distance; if so, this might be the best thing that could come out of a new village. During each Spring Festival, a crowd passes by our front door now and then, as if to revive the long-lost festive mood from years ago. The Spring Festival is the most important tradition in China, and not a time for sorrow. It embodies, and brings alive, all traditional rituals and customs: the display of spring couplets, ancestral worship, visits to relatives, and more. These consist of taboos and rules, which define the beloved local culture and mores. Many of these taboos and rules are allegedly superstitions, but without superstition there is no awe in life, and a people or place without awe is a desolate land of humanity.

I can't help being a witness to the disappearance of some traditional practices in Hengdian, but neither can I do anything about it. I am angry with my own helplessness: like my other self-indulgent compatriots, I have let myself go with this laissez-faire attitude. A disappearance can be irreversible, just as someone dead can never come back to life again. The pain is profound and goes deep into the marrow, as in the case of my mother's death. It is the worst damage inflicted upon a place and its culture, for there is no way for us to find a newer and more efficient substitute culture. In fact, a culture can't be substituted, but it can be improved. We are confronted not by changes but with our regrets for the past. Often I wonder if the reconstruction of our village could improve our living conditions yet preserve our traditional culture. This must be a herculean task. How awkward it must feel to move a memorial tablet into a sparkling clean new house from an old one: in a new, bright house, the deity statue is fully exposed, its mystery lost. Without its mystery, the deity feels reluctant, too. Imagine how much we mortals like some mystery, let alone the gods. Contradictions inevitably exist between tradition and modernity, yet this is not the crux of our problem: our hearts lack respect and awe for heaven and earth and ourselves! Here comes my melancho-lia, the hardest sorrow that I can't rid myself of at present.

So I, too, fall prey to homesickness. My homesickness is not like the nostalgia one feels when observing one's home-town from afar, nor is it poetic nostalgia for the moon or a landscape, one that contains romanticism and sorrow. My homesickness stands on this land and stares blankly at its transformations, helplessness, and victimhood. It reminds me of the heart-wrenching process of watching Mother die, being pushed into the crematorium, and reduced into ash: an eternal and absolute loss. My homesickness is an unresolved melancholia that does not disappear when one returns to one's birthplace, nor is it lyrical. It is bloody and devastat-ingly real. Neither is it "something" one takes from and returns to others: it is an irreplacable piece of bone removed from a body. Certainly, a new bone grows where an old bone has been removed, so what is lost in an old culture may be replaced by the novelties, but these substitutes are pieced together in a raw and hard way; they aren't part of a continu-ity or an expansion. These are the changes that I must con-front directly and every day.

For a while, my mother's death and my love for our home-town, as well as my passivity in response to what comes and goes, exhausted me both mentally and physically: I was afraid that my worries were futile and would hinder me from mov-ing on. I saw how overjoyed my kin were when they moved into their new residence, and how convenient my life became once we moved into our new house. Come the New Year, my father could not bear to paste a couplet on our brand new walls. Neither did he light candles and incense for ancestral workship at our New Year's meal. Just like that, a year passed by sloppily. It felt at once relaxing and bland. Of course I don't know if it is just to say that we now celebrate the New Year plainly, or if we have failed to keep up with rapid changes, just as one can't compare the speed of sedan chairs with bicycles. The so-called plainness isn't about plainness itself, but that we hurry our way through life, and have yet to chew on it carefully, thus wasting its exquisite flavors. Plainness is the challenge one faces when one has to choose among the riches of a material life, and the doubts one faces about what one has chosen to give up.

Likewise, we have chosen to live better and faster in a new village, but we are dubious of what we give up: How many marvels in our old life have we thrown away? Because of doubt and nostalgia, mediocrity becomes a form of excellence, nostalgia an amnesty that in its chaos defines mediocrity as excellence. Whatever isn't deemed as "good," once forgiven and embellished, quietly becomes part of the bigger picture that defines nostalgia. This is an obstacle, but in an impoverished life, one can't be rid of this obstacle, which in itself becomes an essential tool for embellishment. This is why I feel so uncertain about my nostalgia, and can't even deceive myself about it. It is a defeat that shadows me day and night: homesickness in its flesh and blood inflicts an irresistible sense of defeat upon me, rejecting the specious and the superficial, such that one has nowhere to get around.

Still, one goes round and round, like me hoping to find a spot to settle unresolved feelings about my hometown.

I can't tell if others are simply contented with nostalgia, and since they might not return to their hometown, the disappearance of which brings only an impersonal sadness to their inner lives and emotions. Through distance and narratives, their nostalgia has found comfortable remove and space, allowing them to heal their void with other possibilities. No doubt they would deny that the void of their nostalgia could be healed, or insist that it couldn't be replaced. Indeed it can't, but it can be forgotten. What remains is poetic lyricism, a necessity for emotions. Such nostalgia opens their eyes afresh after their grief, but mine can't. Here I am, a witness to the collapse or loss of something concrete, as I stretch my hand out to preserve it, but to no avail. In such instance, my nostalgia is to others a landscape, an irony.

Our anxiety stems from our helplessness, the very passivity and worry that confronts us when we are swept away by this era. We happen to be born in a rapidly advancing age in which changes occur too fast, whereas the origins of our life linger in the slow phase of an agricultural society. We do not know to whom we should shout, *Slow down and wait for me.* No one is waiting. No one waits for our unease and doubts to be appeased. As I write, I feel I have said too much. Rain continues outside, pouring hard on the windowpanes. Loudspeakers nearby are playing a birthday song. I feel blessed nevertheless: a vaguely sad bliss.

Well

Wells are scattered across the ground, if you are drunk
you won't find any
A well dries up, wind rises everywhere
A well brims over, honey seeps out easily
The well, its bewitched kindness and enmity
tighten days brick by brick
Leaked air and rain, a symbolism
Those who draw water vanish in water
The earth is starving and thirsty
Again and again, a girl in a red blouse wipes beads
of bird droppings off the well with her breasts
Clouds echo through her chest

An Afternoon in Hengdian Village

A splendid sun haphazardly shines on sloped roofs, and a row
   of white poplars
shines on a pond, square by square, on its water plants
shines on creeping ferns, rapeseed, wheat

Time isn't flat enough to spread across plants
divided among a cow and ducks in the water
among hand gestures
and me

I use portions of time to gather half a lifetime
Mother uses these fragments to gather a head full of white hair
only the universe rejoices
—it has garnered a spring

In this spring
we merely coat Hengdian Village with new warmth

Listen to a Love Song

I always think of those leaves, how they fall
into silence, a gigantic silence
that silences a village

I think of a quieter setting sun filtered through leaves
those golden sobs
for the sake of a more striking golden

And I think of rain, how it cheers time up
falling
tearing up sorrow, falling straight onto leaves

or on their reverse side
You think of someone, his chest
and back
All in the past. Years drag on
as if they were always there
yet never

If I die, a song will still whirl
If I could still hear it

Leading a Dog's Life

Every afternoon when I mow grass, Little Wu comes along
Sometimes I run after her
while she wags her tail

These days I see a man opposite us harvesting wheat
He yells "Miss Xiuhua" at me with a flattering smile
I mow faster
and cut my finger a few times

A son-in-law lives with his parents-in-law, a wife gone mad
    for twenty·years
Their son suffers from autism
carries a tape recorder around his waist
so loud that a drift pin can hear it

My rabbit runs to another field, Little Wu chases on
but the son's sickle is faster than a dog
After he drags the rabbit home
he is still searching for it

Irrigate the Rapeseed Fields

And they start to argue: she blames him for not doing his part
He claims she only knows how to nag
At noon, the sun scalds their back. Two straw hats tied on water
   pipes, so scaldingly small
yet to swell after sixty years
A sparrow darts past, a shadow shrouds the top of straw hats one by one
not heeding time

You just can't dust off the snow of time
Form is required, it wraps up a wrinkled pit
not to mention the process of revision, blindness and tolerance
A white poplar stretches out a useless branch; he knows the best way
to decorate it is to chop it off
Be careful not to cut anything with a sickle
—she grumbles again

Midnight Village

At this instant, a lamp must be glowing on your imagination
A dejected woman must be hesitating over a sheet of writing paper
You strain to recall the village
let alone on this rainy night

Obviously she won't reply to your letter
She can't find words for this interrogation
—their child is in the pond, they're fishing out his corpse
She is speechless, but her mind is set

He lives in Beijing: for ten years, he doesn't know
a lump grows in her breast
He insists, *You're mine*
when he phones from a foot massage parlor

Quiet before her child's tomb, she sheds not a tear that night
He has no idea how much land has gone to waste in the village
How her heart has gone cold
he too has no idea

Background

After rounds of rain, a tree grows thin
The sun is out, on dark, moldy leaves
How unattractive
Such a blue sky to cover Hengdian Village
Such white clouds to drift over white poplars
Newly planted barley flicks out a coat of furry green
Weeds wither out a gripping hour
I sit in a field, autumn wind enters my bosom
Sparrows crew by crew, down and up in a swirl
falling on a telephone line over the crops, so softly
not bearing to alarm sporadic news from afar

Gratitude

Sunlight falls on eaves and white poplars
and an azure-winged magpie on the second branch
It falls on its dazzling white belly

I sit on a stoop
A cat on another, dozing off
tilting its head here
and there

Between us sunlight enters our main room
The pendulum clock seems to pause
and goes on to sway
a trivial voice

A Woman on the Rooftop

This afternoon, the breeze whitens a flock of water birds
an afternoon before a pond of reeds nervously withers
an afternoon when a magpie stands on a white poplar
an afternoon when a tangerine is forgotten on a branch
This is a woman's afternoon: she stands on a rooftop
watches an afternoon float and shimmer

She watches passersby on the boulevard
No one sees her
She hears them converse loudly or softly
No one knows she can hear
She reckons someone will walk out of the crowd to wave at her
No one knows what she reckons

In the village where she lived all her life
she feels so close
to the sky again

The Swaying Mortal World

I HAVE LONG BELIEVED THAT fatalism begins when you connect intimately with certain things and fall so hard in love with them that it becomes impossible for you to give them up. Take me, for instance: I love and suffer in poetry, rejoice over poetry while pursuing it, not to mention the untold dejection—poetry connects my emotions in ways that nothing else can. I throw myself into life, persevere, and look forward to what lies ahead. I am grateful that poetry exists in my life: it presents me as I am; it shields me.

Indeed, when I first thought to express my feelings through language, I chose poetry because of my cerebral palsy. Writing a word is strenuous for me: I must exert all my strength to balance my body, pressing my right wrist down with my left hand before struggling to get a word out. Among all literary genres, poetry uses the least amount of words. Naturally, it spoke best to me.

Still, my first verses weren't exactly poetry: they merely allowed me to enjoy the pleasure of my favorite words. How overjoyed I was when I filled an entire notebook with my distorted words. When I asked my teacher to take a look at my diary in verse, he replied in writing, "You're such a charming girl: the odds and ends of your life have turned into poetry." These simple words moved my heart: having someone praise me as charming was all that I could ask for. I set out to keep this charm with me all my life, and sure enough, I have managed to do so.

As far as I am concerned, I feel complete, calm, and happy only when I am writing a poem. I have never been a calm person: I have no desire to resign myself to fate, nor can I bow down to it meekly. Having exhausted all forms of resistance, I yell and curse in public. Of course, I am but a peasant woman who can't quite mend her bad ways. Never have I imagined poetry as a weapon; even if it might work as one, I wouldn't wield it—my love for poetry is too strong. Much as society might contaminate my mind, poetry cleanses me with compassion.

I never think about how to write poetry, or what I should write. When I panic about my personal life, I find myself unable to care for my country or mankind. I explore these subjects in writing, either because they have stirred me or brought me sorrow and anxiety. The fact that one lives a good life speaks volumes about the inherent well-being of one's society, and vice versa. Any social tolerance bestowed upon me, a distinctly disabled person, will mirror the yardstick for a healthy society. This is why I believe that as long as I live in earnest, my poetry will glow in earnest.

Tonight, for example, I am writing these thoughts on poetry in a rowdy Internet café. No one knows my inner joy and calm. In the provincial training squad where I trained as a competitive chess player, I was the most reticent member. I did not need words. Rather, I was more eager to gaze at the sky alone. At my age, too much has been said. Yet poetry has stayed close to me, and never rejects me when I think of it. But what poetry is, I don't know, nor can I speak of it. It is simply an emotion that leaps or drowns. It comes in the guise of a patriotic pose when the soul summons it. It is just a cane for one who staggers in a swaying mortal world.

I Tripped in the Afternoon

Carrying a basket over a ditch, I fell
A basket of grass fell, too
So did a sickle
Shoes on the brambles, hanging on the brambles
a white scarf
In case I hurt my hands, I brought along a light white scarf
to bind them up
But ten years have passed, it's still so white
Where is the man who gave me the white scarf
These thoughts came to me when I fell: eyes wide open
clouds looked majestically white
grass scattered all over, majestically green

Dust

Yes, it can't stand on its own, so it leans west in the wind
Water shadows overlap, how can you trust a
drowned person
Time and again, she tries to fish light and honey
out from her body
The drowned bears the weight of a rock. She blows bubbles
to bend, shatter, and fade light out
—a process never rectified
She can only blow with what she has
at the overdrafts of life
—this is also an irreversible process
but let's forgive her
She drags the remote far into her body, it still holds an impenetrable fear

A Pool of Water

My favorite moment: dusk darkens, night still young

My soul so clear, tumbling on a leaf

A lamp and shadow: I live naked, my shadow stretches itself

a segment kept to feed its silhouette

Water surges from everywhere and disperses everywhere

Softly I sway in water

carry luminous words at the tip of grass

I like to be besieged by verses, to find a way out by working my heart out

Something loves me, it never leaves me

Yet it can't flow

or find a summit in a song

Our goats are young, their bleating soft. A hundred steps

away from summer fruits

we must have lived to know such a moment

to see a part we ignore in ourselves

Rain Falls outside the Window

But I kept staying on the spot where I dried, drank a bottle of wine
flipped and pushed it over, put it upright
then pushed it over
Rain outside the window neglected me: a drop hugged another, fell
and pushed each other, falling
Fusion is wreckage, wreckage fusion
But how long can one return to the sky, how long does it take to reach
a descent
—when I flick a speck of cigarette ash, another has arisen
I love someone to death
Another is in my belly
Rain sounds different in different places
No one vanishes faster than another
No one arrives more compact than another
No one in the rain, or not in it

Two Voices Late at Night

My deep night contains two voices
a haunted soul's yell
Yu Xiuhua's lament

I love two men
one has left
the other never comes

My morning holds two rows of light
one shines as I write
another as I bathe

Wriggle

After breakfast, I walk to the village
and back

Sometimes I stop awhile, sometimes I don't
Sometimes I hope to meet the one I have a crush on, sometimes I hope
I don't

Slowing down will prolong this part of my journey
I see a roadside reed, facing south, a second reed, a third . . .
The plain is deep at this time

Today for instance, an abrupt wind grows on my way home
Water in a fish pond flaps against the bank, spouting white ripples

Wriggling like soft snow
I'm so close to winter

But Not for Me

Only this slightness can destroy me, only this pain
can't yell

Hugging my knees at midnight, I listen to withering: not just roses
but night itself, the milky way
a cosmos

—I don't know who to call for help
A breach in life: distant tides a disastrous defeat

This is how I get through my nights: tearing flowers into pieces
—I doubt my love, it shatters us each time
I doubt my inborn defect: a destructive nature

No matter what, I'm not cut out for him
I believe love exists for him and others
but not for me

Hillfolk

You get me drunk and say a crowd gathers in town, but I'm thinking
   of a mountain locust tree
You get me drunk and say someone has invited me to dance,
   but I'm thinking of a mountain locust tree bare of leaves

I only praise
the sun on me, a squirrel's hole north of locust trees, its frantic mother

I'm the one who climbs uphill with rain on my back, in the past and future
I'm the one with dark clouds in my arms, in the past and future

When you see me, I'm a pile of mud
When you see me, wind scatters fallen leaves, I'm a pile of damp mud

Hanging Rock

Still, I was startled—my face at once awash with tears
Overwhelmed by grief, I went round the rock and back
For days, silence pressed on silence
my body pieced by ash, my heart molded by sunset

So risky, so heavy
O this love

I Live to Reject
Lofty Words

1

First word: *Suffering.*

This year, I have had the opportunity to visit several different places and have met many journalists and poetry friends. During interviews or after my talks, they would ask questions such as, "How did you transform your suffering into poetry? How do you approach suffering in life?"

Suffering is indeed a fascinating word. It implies that one who has suffered is a person worthy of respect, so his or her outlook on life can't be "wrong." Suffering is suffering because it seeks truth. To some degree, it also suggests that since one has endured a life of suffering, one will be forgiven for any wrongdoing. After prolonged suffering, how many can still maintain a lucid mind and not succumb to self-pity?

Although I respect the word *suffering*, I am skeptical of it whenever someone tells me that my life defines *suffering*.

Yes, life is bitter and has its challenges, but it isn't disastrous. As long as one is still alive, I can't see how life is a disaster. One has the right to choose, either to escape or to commit suicide, and is compelled by no one to live in this world.

The fact that suffering can be transformed into poetry is in itself a feat. Suffering can propel and motivate one to write. On the other hand, suffering is suffering nonetheless. Writing about it can neither alleviate nor alter it. Writing merely provides us a form of expression, much as suffering is palpable and present.

Sometimes, I suffer so much that no one can help me, and this drives me to despair. Despair exists because hope has existed, even if it is usually a desire for the impossible. Many times I reassure myself that I am still alive and kicking, that I have food and clothes . . . so this should suffice. I shouldn't quibble over minor details, after all, one shouldn't be greedy.

There is so much suffering in this world. Suffering is deep-rooted, and its roots easily located, but this fact is hardly any consolation to anyone. Our suffering lies in the brevity of our life, and the value of our life cannot be measured by its very own transience. In this respect, suffering seeks what life can't find; for that, one should give thanks to one's fate.

How I wish I could ask, *What criteria does one use to judge my life as suffering?* My physical disability, to begin with? Yes, *disability* is a word one can't ignore. It controls one's body and changes the orientation of one's inner life. I believe the human body is like an experimental sample that provides us with multiple versions and aspects of a soul.

Undeniably, a disabled body is a great inconvenience in life, and leaves no room for all kinds of possibilities. But it is also fair to say that the disabled body's soul does not feel about the external world any less than others. This is what counts most. True joys come from the depth of one's soul, not the external environment.

Still, melancholia exists because of a mounting lack of sensitivity and understanding, along with physical pain and problems. There is grief that one can't deny. Having endured this much hardship, I still know of a sorrow that follows me like a shadow. Is this misery? Hardly. After all, how can one be totally free from sorrow?

This is why I don't think I have much "suffering" to share with others. It is unlikely for one to find, in my work and life, ways to get rid of suffering. All I want to do is to live on with a fiery gaze and my teeth clenched.

2

Second word: *Strength.*

This is not a disparaging word. Nor is it flattering when used regarding a woman or a disabled woman. Linguistically, it is hard and indifferent. It is a word that stares out blankly, and long enough to make one feel nervous and disgusted.

What can be more natural than Life itself? Imposed on one's body, the word *strength* bears no specific connotation. Who is more deserving of this word? Those who have suffered hardship, such as me. I fit the criteria too well: I am a disabled woman who lives in a poor village and suffers an unhappy marriage. Further, my mother has recently fallen ill. To be frank, I am at a loss, and often can't help but weep. I have even imagined a new life in which I could run away from this world.

But what can I do? Nothing, absolutely nothing. I don't want to die, so I must live. As long as I stay alive, I will take on all my suffering. I have no other choice but to accept this passively. Unless one is a lunatic, no one takes on hardship willingly. And this is how I learn to be strong.

The adjective *strong* is intended as praise, but who does it praise other than someone drenched in blood? It has nothing to do with an award, but with the attitude one adopts, even if one does so unwillingly.

A strong woman is essentially an unfortunate being who can't lean on others for help. In a way, her life is a failure. Fortunately, neither success nor failure is shameful or shocking in life: because of a failed life, her life lies right before her own eyes. We do not live to show others what our lives are, nor do we live to please anyone.

Strength is, therefore, about ourselves; it mirrors our inner life and does not take into account others' opinions and conceit. We persevere in doing what we like, and the more we persevere, the stronger we become.

I suppose when others praise us as strong, we should acknowledge them with silence. There is nothing to argue about, nor do we need others to understand our misery. One's experience can't serve as a role model for others, nor should it exist as a subject for others to lament.

Please don't tell me how strong I am. I am just surviving with my thick skin, not to mention my dull life.

3

Third word: *Role model*.

After meeting people from all walks of life, one has naturally witnessed a variety of arguments, both critical and encouraging. Right or wrong, people relish in judging and defining others in words. Over and over, for instance, I hear others say, *Professor Yu, you're our role model*.

Their remark makes me sweat: am I not just a peasant woman who happens to have written two, three poems? How then can I be a "role model" for others? This explains my skepticism about being a "role model."

I have never had a role model who serves as my inspiration. If my past was considered lousy because I never had a role model in my younger days, then let it be so.

Lei Feng, for example, was never my role model, neither was Zhang Haidi. When I was in elementary school, I went out of my way to buy a copy of *Lei Feng's Diary*, but the book left me nonplussed. My teacher claimed that I was Zhang

Haidi reincarnated. Immediately, I jumped up and protested, "I am Yu Xiuhua, not Zhang Haidi." I couldn't know where my urge to resist began, but I did tell myself that I would never blindly follow in their footsteps—my journey in life must be different from theirs.

Whenever I meet other disabled people, their family members come up to ask me, *Yu Xiuhua, how do you persevere in such difficult conditions? Can you give us some advice?*

My honest answer: I have no advice.

Indeed I have none, to say nothing of the opportunities and life I am blessed with. Obviously, I can't survive without putting in due effort. So here is my word: labor! Labor sums up my outlook on life, and has nothing to do with being a role model. Barring chance, necessity, or history, I am incapable of any advice or suggestions.

Every life is unique. My life can't serve as a role model for another's. I believe you can influence others through your outlook on life, which can have a positive impact through your resilience and self-scrutiny. This is a spiritual practice that cannot be influenced by something like a role model.

I don't believe in the power of a "role model," and I don't wish to be one. I don't know if I've ever wanted to be one, but when you become a role model, you become sad and skeptical: your life will soon be "duplicated" elsewhere. How dreadful.

More often than not, we feel helpless in face of genuine suffering. Faced with concrete aspects of suffering in a mundane life, a role model pulls himself or herself back. The idea of a "role model" sounds poetic, but life is a tangible abyss of suffering. Sometimes we do not even know what to do with ourselves, let alone how to influence others.

People need a role model because they have no idea what to do in times of anguish. They can't find an effective solution, so they need a reference. Once they imagine they have found a plausible reference at last, they might realize how futile it is.

Let me say to these people: read more. Reading is a powerful activity: it calms one's heart. When the mind is quiet, one can experience real joy. Regardless of our unbearable bodies or lives, we are each unique in this world. We ought to cherish ourselves. So why ask for more?

I don't know if these words seem unwarranted, but since I am no one's role model, I can allow myself to talk nonsense.

4

Fourth word: *Purpose*.

Ultimately, one discovers in life a process instead of a *purpose*. If some purpose exists in life, what could it be? The end of life is death, which has nothing to do with life in itself. In each life, purposes big or small abound by and large, yet life itself bears no purpose.

Because there exists no one purpose in life, we feel a constant void. Nothing but life itself can enter our lives. No matter how hard we try, all our endeavors seem dissipated, unable to find their focus point. What a frightening reality. Yet no one knows the afterlife, whether it exists in a similar or greater void. So all we can do is to get by in life, one day at a time.

Life is not an end in itself. Why do we carry on, trapped in power, glory, and loss? Perhaps it is a game to fight emptiness in a tedious life. Now and then, I find nothing worthy of love in our world and can't wait to disappear, but in a split second I change my mind: death is predestined, so one need not be impatient; even when we lose all of our dignity and fortune, life will continue to toy with us.

Problems find their resolution when they can't be solved. Life is not an end, so let's live with lighter spirits. There is a saying, "Man should lead a well-lived life that soars," but what a herculean mission that is. Each society has its own order, which to some extent restricts us and our lives, since one can't be entirely separated from one's social attributes.

In my opinion, the purpose of life is life itself, just as love is its own purpose. Hatred does not exist for no reason, but love, yes. Things that exist for no reason or purpose tend to be beautiful: they are the essence of purity, and purity the essence of happiness. Modern civilization has brought us material convenience but has hurt our spiritual life.

This applies to poetry: any writing that serves a purpose is a dubious activity. For me, writing can't be the intent to write. I write poetry simply because I enjoy writing poems. Why write? Enjoyment is the reason and purpose. Poetry is about expressing what one wishes to share with others, and life a matter of living a life as one wishes.

Much as there exists no specific purpose in life, we can create a myriad of "trivial" purposes: completing a manuscript, for example, or enjoying the scenery. These "trivialities" in life bring pleasure to one's mind and body, even if they seem devoid of meaning. One can't believe how all sorts of "efficient" behavior could, too, end up as part of an "inefficient" life, yet such absurdity is what renders life its subtle logic.

I am desperately in love with this inexplicable and obscure life. I love its conceit, and the haze that surfaces at low points in my life. I am grateful for being well and alive, and all because of my lowly existence.

All You Need Is to Be Alive

All you need is to be alive, God has His own plans. I watch Japanese
   honeysuckle sprout
Fine weather: each cloud an alien in a foreign sky
For years I've longed to escape from my hometown, betray this village
   called Hengdian
Yet time and again fate keeps me here, where I guard a shabby hut,
   my old parents
and a son soon grown-up
My son, like a slow approaching guest, slowly draped in my odor

Bliss is this, just nicely this
Overwhelmed and discreet, I can't even say a word
To live like a part of a shadow, fallen from the sky into water
Couples who stay together all their lives fail to love, end up living alone
Who stops us from saying *No!* to such life

Here comes February, the word *live* comes alive
Every day I clean the house for a clean sun to enter
I grow Chinese roses, let them blossom again and again
I keep a rabbit, give it a den
She can't turn her back on life even when she is unhappy (I'm her life,
   in which tenderness and cruelty coexist)

More often I just survive, not ill, no desire, one meal each day
I have lived into the *future*, thus is the future
Slowly a plant's heart grows in the body
What a surprise, yet how naturally

A Leaky Boat

Secrets or origins untraced by history
omit the trouble of lies through a snowstorm

For forty years, it's been coaxed back by a larger wave to the shallow area
It plays with fish and shrimp
A gifted wind hunter that catches wind language, a snake in a cup

The boat has just endured two voids
One leaks out its body into a starry sky in the lake
Another leaks into the fish in its body

Starry night, again a starry night, the fish are nowhere
A fish doesn't know a man has come
and left traces in the boat

This is the only boat that confesses to being a boat
on a desolate shore
the nature of wood from a past life, and water of this time

Wheat in a Threshing Ground

May aims for a place, strikes from the sky
falls off high clouds after a long dream
onto a golden survival

My father turns wheat over again
—a heart's inner moisture must aim for sunlight
so wheat won't turn moldy in winter
After turning it over, he pinches a grain
and bites it hard
so moonlight flows aground

If I swam among wheat in this threshing ground
I'd rinse my body of details
and lyrical adjectives
afraid that my frail bones
couldn't endure such gold

Marvels

To love you, I learn tenderness, slow-boil sweet words
No matter what, I want to hug you, to leap and kiss you

Sigh, why do you attract me: a beard with lice
You aren't April, even October has passed
Bedroom matters aren't always a bed of roses
Only a disappointing woman like me has placed all goodness on you
has even thought of stealing or snatching

—as if beauty in this world was just for you and your enjoyment
Roses aren't enough, nor orchards, nor flowing water and clouds
Spring isn't enough
Can you guess if I might trip on my way to stealing something
Ah, Heavens, how marvelous, don't say it aloud
Ah, if I went missing
you must look through your body: does a striking scar
ache for no reason

A Day Bestowed by God

Morning glories lift blue up a fence, as wind blows from afar
A lush growth—
each flavor penetrates me, warm and sweet

I stand in the vast plain and see your city
in its radiance
I know you've crossed the road with a basket of apples

All clues are here
A day bestowed by God: you and I, content with the mortal world
What a precious gift

Gift

1

To my astonishment, I realize: when one feels bliss, bliss has quietly arrived. And at this very moment, bliss has virtually metaphormosed into a talent or an ability. Yet this ability isn't the cumulative process of one's efforts to achieve something, nor is it a force, thought, or technique that one can exercise. Quite the contrary: it is about putting aside metaphysical work, and observing this specific instant as a bystander. Everything is let go, not a grain of sand in one's hand; one feels calm between Heaven and Earth. When one can let go of everything, the process in itself is an achievement.

To be frank, I don't know what I have or can let go. Perhaps I haven't let go of anything at all. Luckily, this does not affect my happiness: the sun shines right into the courtyard, on old tiles, the roof, and drooping corrugated tiles; a few sparrows leap here and there, on the rooftop or in the courtyard. The sun is dynamic: once sparrows flutter their wings, sunlight will diffuse in circles, interwoven with light from elsewhere, before getting entangled in one. A subtle yet heavy sound arises from the backyard, where an old towel is left to dry, its colors so faded that one can hardly see it. But once I catch sight of it, I feel at ease, as if time were drying on a vine where moldy spots and loopholes are exposed to the sun.

I love this instant from the bottom of my heart. My love for this marvelous instant has never ceased, from when I first experienced it. It must have consoled me on countless occasions when I have felt sad, lost, and ignorant; it must have been quietly giving me hope, and the strength to jump out of bed every day. To love sunshine and nature is part of our human nature. It will never let us stay far from nature for too long.

At this point, if I want to indulge further in this marvelous moment, I will brew a cup of tea, switch on my computer, create a brand new document, and let words leap, one by one, on the page. Of course, even though these words aren't exactly arranged in a satisfying way, I can't help but feel pleased with the black characters on a blank page.

People often ask, *Why do you write, and what does writing mean to you?* The truth is, one does not need a reason to like someone or something. I can't tell if the so-called reason leads to any inexplicable purpose. When I like something—I mean, truly like—it tends to be related to some intrinsic attribute, the chromosomes of life. To me, the means of writing is its own end! One can derive enough joys from writing itself. The thrill of writing far surpasses the joys of publication. This is the only reason why one can keep on writing one's whole life long.

I thank God for my desire to write: this desire exists just as joy exists.

2

Why write?

If I don't respond—casually but candidly—with the simple reason "Because I like it," the question might evolve into a roundabout philosophical subject. I don't see a need to make a big fuss about philosophy, which is merely a generic title not responsible for the things it names. I naughtily believe that I am not necessarily responsible for my own words, since I might, too, be engaging in "philosophy" as a way to answer some of my questions in life.

I believe in life in its indubitable essence. I go for the easy approach that considers a meal, power, poverty, and wealth as analogous. I mean, if all of us take life seriously, and make a go of it, Heaven will bless us with wealth all the same: joy—like the joy I experience in the sun.

Yes, writing eradicates difference: not just the parity in wealth or so-called social status, but psychological differences such as differing sensory perceptions of bliss. In my opinion, this is a fundamental human difference. To gauge bliss is to gauge one's love for an ordinary life.

Writing is a spiritual practice. In general, I think those who become disillusioned with the mortal world, and hide in monasteries to practice Buddhism, adopt a somewhat evasive approach to life. Surely a practice isn't an escape but a profound understanding, a kind of *seeing through*. Some say poetry is disparate from life. How? I don't know. This sort of response seems no different from a superficial liking for poetry. Words are after all one's daily thoughts.

I don't fancy the idea of writing "for" one's life. This sounds like putting the cart before the horse. Life is the eternal foundation. If writing can redeem life, that must be an act destined by God's will: the awakening of oneself to redeem lost years. Until now, I have never thought of writing as my redemption. Writing is in my nature; even if I had to beg, I wouldn't give it up. When I was working in Wenzhou, I had neither a computer nor a desk, so I just sprawled on the bed and scribbled through half a notebook. This has nothing to do with being strong or penniless. I enjoy writing, plain as that.

The poorest life isn't one lacking in material wealth but one without a concrete hobby. What a scary life, I think. I am grateful to God for my literary hobby. I find in it such concrete joy—what a marvelous gift.

3

I have wondered why I am thrust into the public eye, and why many have since embraced or come to know about my work. Why has the spotlight suddenly shifted onto me, someone who does not even play a minor role in life? What virtue do I have? What am I capable of? Once I think about these questions, I will stop detesting those who have humiliated or insulted me. After all, these are the miseries I ought to endure. They have come to me during a dense period in my life, and I panic because they have perhaps come at a wrong time. Still, they are doomed to come.

And I have started to doubt myself: I have done hardly any good deeds, and as for honors, I am afraid I am not fit for them. I survive merely on my own, yet this solitude comes with some indignation. I can only speak truthfully at all times, not that I don't wish to say untruthful things, but if I did, I would feel conscience-stricken, as if I had treated myself poorly. Might God be aware of my actions? Or has He been too compassionate?

In 2013, I broke out of my complicated life and emotions but still couldn't free myself of them. I knew the crux of my problems and their solutions, but the main issue was my reluctance: I had thought of my disability as a destructive force in my life—it destroyed the life I could have enjoyed. At that time, I had the intention of not just insulting others, but of killing them, too. Of course I ended up killing myself. What to do? I must still live on, telling myself that I must live on for now and *see* how things turn out, even if I had no idea what I could *see*.

By chance, I began to write fiction. I don't write a lot every day: just two thousand words, but I keep at it regularly. After a while, I feel better, for no apparent reason, and learn to let go. I must have found self-redemption through literature. Writing gives me the opportunity to know myself anew: *Admit that your disability has given you everything!* By putting myself to order through words, I confront myself again: *You are disabled, and God has given your disability to strip you of your possible "bliss."* But is my idea of bliss actually bliss? Or jealousy of others for what they have and that I have not? Time and again I examine myself, consider things that I can take on in life, and integrate them within the entire setup of Life. I thought, *Fine, this is what I should endure. God has given me a wounded body. There is no reason why I shouldn't shoulder some hardship for its sake.*

4

This morning—January 21, 2016—the sun shines again and splendidly so. Yesterday, someone predicted a heavy snowfall for today, but as it turns out, what a magnificent day! My son is hiding in his bed, playing with his cell phone. I woke up early to wash our clothes and dry them outside. I might as well take the rest of our unwashed clothes outside to dry, too. Then I obliged a friend who had asked me to write him a verse: *Let poetry and love sing aloud on this vast land.* He mentioned that I could express myself as freely as I wished, but I thought these few words would suffice. Poetry and love, I believe, forever sing aloud on this vast land, no matter how traumatic it might seem.

This year, I was away from home at least twice a month, sometimes for as long as several weeks. Poetry has given me the opportunity to travel far and wide. I never could have imagined that it possesses such power. I can't deny that its force surpasses my imagination. Through me, poetry reveals its value: it is acknowledged and accepted by others. Because of my work, many non-poetry-readers have started to read poetry, and now, I can at last affirm a little of my value: I have brought poetry out from my home! So whenever I experience mixed reception of my work, I feel indifferent.

Someone has asked me, *You've been to so many places this year, so how has this changed your views and style of writing?* It hasn't, actually. The essence of poetry is its inward travel. If external changes reach the point of inducing inner changes, it would then bring about changes in poetry. To this day, I still can't commit myself to superficial gatherings. The world and its changes merely serve as a reference for self-examination. One can't expect external changes to change oneself. Why might one appeal to others—no doubt this has to do with one's inner disposition, and how one exudes it, which is unique. We know too well that our outside world centers too much on things in common, which is why it loses its own appeal.

I never expect myself to be capable of appealing to others. I have found this rather shallow. I need to appeal to myself, be affectionate with myself, before ending my long days in solitude. This wish of mine is the best gift for myself.

Lesser Spear Grass

THE LOCALS CALL IT *BROKEN bamboo green.* I prefer this name, too, as it is simpler and more visual. Life and experience speak right to the heart of objects, animals, or plants. Lesser spear grass is a weed. In summer, it interweaves majestically among crops, but is generally not found in rice fields. Instead, it grows among dry upland crops such as cotton, peanuts, and corn.

A broken bamboo green has no grievance about being a weed. Naturally, it isn't a weed from the outset, and is only identified as such by crop growers. I imagine that even if it were aware of being named a weed, it would not feel inferior. A weed might even feel God's presence more than we do. God rejoices because of the weed's presence, so the weed rejoices in return. The Bible says, "See how the lilies of the field grow; they do not sow or reap or store away in barns, and yet your heavenly Father feeds them." God appears to render all existence natural and without discrimination. No difference exists between the privileges of fate, whereas privileges discriminate in life. With difference comes inequality; with inequality come resistance and struggle. God seems to have forgiven the weed for its resistance and struggle, as it has neither mortal solitude nor anxiety. If we humans each possess a peaceful mind, we will not fight for anything in life. Life, however, may turn stale. So if someone is ever jealous of you, and fights with you in life, pity them.

Naive plants boast of a robust vitality. They need no plan to know that once born, they must multiply and survive with all that they have. This is nature, and needs no explanation. Their minds are focused on proliferation and nothing more. As for crops, because of their artificially cultivated genes, they have lost some natural attributes, which in turn renders them weaker in a natural environment. For instance, they have lost the spirit of battling against nature and so think only of flowering; even when the time is not yet right, they are often caught by weeds in their own footsteps. Only natural things find the fastest way to attain life. It goes without saying that others need to pay a higher price to reap more because they ask for more.

Of all weeds, lesser spear grass is especially tenacious. It does not care for anything, and pounces on any hope it finds. When we hoe grass, our parents will nag us about where to look for weeds, where to pay more attention . . . lest weeds turn green and wild everywhere in a few days. Obviously, we can't win over weeds. Sometimes, by chance, a frail root falls onto the water, and when dewdrops emerge, the weed will sprout out its tiny green brain. How discouraging and depressing. Still, it pops out and multiples happily, as if it has never known pain or destruction.

A weed's tenacity depends on the purity of its pride. No pride arises out of thin air; it has its roots and foundation, self-knowledge, and trust in its land. Pride is a silent action: it despises you when you rush to cut grass, yet cannot find its roots. Well, its roots are hidden deep in its own heart; of course, it won't be an easy feat to find them. Sincere and frank, pride says, *Just shovel on, I have no grievance, you simply can't deprive me of my right to grow.* Possibly because of its candor and tolerance, it continues to strive in our world.

Ever so green, it must have been nourished by fertilizers in the land. I have never seen lesser spear grass wilt. It also brings people joy at first sight. A weed is a weed just because it grows in the wrong place by mistake, and its existence hinders others' growth . . . unintentionally. Or perhaps it conforms to a specific order: the samsara of eternal life. What do a few deaths matter? Death is no more than a recurring and necessary path. If a weed grew in a flowerpot, or, say, without hindrance on a crop ridge, it could appear as an enticing stretch of scenery. I feel less ashamed when I manage to restrict the scope of its growth to crop fields.

Although I pull weeds out of the crops, I have never thought of myself as doing something wrong. It would be disingenous of me to claim that I shouldn't have thought or done so. On the other hand, the act of pulling weeds out is in accordance with the existing order of nature. Although we are enemies to some extent, I like weeds and the colors as they grow, without complaint or lament. Life is here, joy is too eager to arrive. A weed has no desire to waste time on sighs. And me? Do I treasure life as it does? No, not at all!

But life, like Zen, may not bring on immediate enlightenment. Nonetheless, life never fails to offer us the way of nature. Tao is the way, and all things come along with the path. A wide path is invisible. The invisible enhances life and its immensity. Given such revelation, all questions will vanish in days to come, and silence will be the final answer to all questions. I don't see a better way, or a higher intelligence than this. There is no better ode to life than a weed that grows ruthlessly and arches out of the ground, despite its trauma.

There is a word in our language and culture, *grass-folks*, which refers to ordinary people who survive like ants and creeping vines on the ground. This word very much contains the disdain for a certain social class. Fortunately, contempt hurts only the slanderers themselves, who suffer from misunderstandings based on their judgment. Those creeping vines continue to rejoice, living each day meticulously and earnestly. One may say that such a day is small and insignificant, but broadly speaking, no one day is bigger than another.

Yet those who are wounded or trampled upon at any time are precisely the ones capable of holding up the sky of history, and of tolerating drastic changes and the pain of history, so the genes of a culture and civilization can seep through the soil and be preserved. But an ordinary citizen can't think this far: he worries nonstop about his daily life, in hope of a better day even when this day will never arrive. A strand of weed can't imagine spring in its bones, nor can it work out the significance of its own contribution to spring. All it wishes is to stay forever green: it has no other mission or wish.

The vitality of lesser spear grass can be annoying: it never ceases to gather in itself force and willpower, saying, *I am invincible. My greenness is inexhaustible. I want to be worthy of my green.* This is why we can't pull weeds as fast as they grow. Man will invariably be defeated by a strand of weed. There is no room for chicanery. In the end, my father must resort to pesticides to tame weeds. But a weed looks down on banal pesticides, save for the most powerful Paraquat that wipes it all out, before the weed returns to life years later. One dies upon consuming Paraquat: there is no antidote.

Only Paraquat can kill lesser spear grass. If one forgets to use the pesticide, the weed will burst out again, unexpectedly. How terrifying. I feel ashamed when I stand before it. We are so remote from death, yet tortured beyond recognition by life itself. Li Po states, "Every talent has its place or time." I consider being alive most purposeful. One's existence is a heritage in itself, and the radiance of one's insignificant thoughts must have inadvertently enlightened others one way or another.

Dusk behind the Mountain

A warm setting sun: sitting on a mound, you see running water beneath
A child can go downhill and wash twilight years
How wonderful, kites and butterflies with somewhere to go
A cow nibbling at grass seems like an interlude

If one insists on a unique day
it must be today: a tomb grows on a mound
Crows panic and fall one by one
Grass keeps on wilting

No matter how dense the mud is, I enter
softly
Bargaining in the past now seems like a joke
Jaws exercise nonstop, as if to chew life into pieces

I sit until the sky turns starry and say, *Let's go home*
Longtime terrified, a strand of grass
twitches
in an indistinct wind

Short

Wheat is short, so are yellow bok choy
If wind doesn't sweep grass low
Father who sits by the field with a rice bowl will miss it
Sparrows swirl around awhile, then fall
He says, *Grasshoppers can't jump high whatever the season*

Not to mention weeds and flowers, those with a straw hat
Clouds are short, so are poplars
But how tall are poplars at human height
seen yet ignored

Short things can't be blown away
Father's sixty years, my thirty-eight

Gardenias in Bloom

Whitening into a havoc, fragrance a disaster
Covert voices push their way out layer by layer, a pile redisperses
    layer by layer
Yes, speechless
White isn't a color, but a posture

Every year, abrupt as scheduled: existence seen as an expression
Gorgeous and here anyway
enduring a waning solitude: radiant
not turning back

Where does the force of a gush come from? It refuses moonlight
opens anytime, yes, it opens itself
in pain
so painfully that it can't cry out
Fire licking its roots, water falling off a leaf
the gaze of things on earth
all white
unstoppable, desperately

I'll Sing Every Spring

Every spring I'll sing, watch clouds arrive from the south
Once wind softens, spring gets real

A man sits on a ridge where dandelions carry small flames
running in spring, all the way out of the village
He can't hear my voice

I want to call him, I have things unsaid
Too brief a flowering, too short a time for spring to rest
He shouts, *I can't hear you properly, can't hear you*

He can't hear a cerebral palsy patient's muffled confession
Many pass by spring, many flowers in bloom
He can't guess what I'm saying

But I'll sing every spring
A voice sways in the wind, sad and sweet

Temptation

He takes off spring in the morning. Flowers shut, even light
walks deep into autumn

Fallen leaves beat on his shoulders: shudder, a temptation
like his silence
Sunset penetrates his ankles: meandering light, a temptation
like his smile

Even at dusk, he washes himself in a river
the stains on his body

When he opens a wooden box, butterflies
and bees rush into his face, along with an erected hive
and
his calm and quiet

May • Wheat

They ambush me, hoist fire in the day, flow as water at night
They are attached to what I am attached to: voles, crickets, sparrows
a straw man in Grandpa's clothes

Sincere and frank, at the heart of a wheat field, I bear the burden
    of love, its coming and going
kin coming and going
Low eaves, ready to shelter wheat from rain

Departure as arrival, I clean my body by the river
Strong and plump, she replenishes herself
with moonlight and empties it out

I, a farmer shy away from expressing my feelings for wheat with a pen
    and ink
I can just put it in my mouth
chew the process of autumn to summer
slowly gulp it down, fill up my mortal troubles
build a strand of wheat's counterencirclement
with a clear conscience

Past a Cemetery

Like stars at dusk, glittering. Walking in a cemetery, the fired-up me
secretly expands in my body, an unruly fire
Wind sways, holds onto fire, extinguishes me once it grows

They gaze at me a planet apart. Those on the front line of time
fall asleep for my sake, suck half the world into the soil
So I stumble here and there, my flesh cut, blood shed

Yet in each instance, I'm struck
hoping to find harsh reproach in incessant whispers
Only wind—howling from the mouth of an empty wine bottle

until nightfall, when even the nearest tomb is buried
my suddenly empty body
untouched by universal gravitation

On the Plain

Not without a tree, or a house
If a train passes, houses run out
Mobile components: ants, pigs, misguided crows
A mortal world, densely or sparsely populated
In this late spring cold, rain falls on a plain, meandering chimney
   smoke disperses on the spot

Morning fog everywhere: when a train stops at a station
he sees a woman sneak out from her back door
A red skirt sways in the wind
A red scar between her eyebrows: protruding beauty and wreckage
He sees her walk into a tree hole, a ball of fog drifting out

He's unaware she has done a painting in a tree hole
She has painted a thick fog, the train yellow
A man smokes and looks around outside the window. A tree
   exists in his eyes
This happens all the time: beaten black and blue by her husband
she would hide in a tree hole and paint

Longing for a Snowstorm

I long for heavy snowfall, without premeditation, denser than death
Unexpectedly, in a deluge, smashing hatred down

I need it to be this violent. My slightness isn't a snowfall
a careless reason

I want the whiteness I loathe to pile on top of me! In this vast wasteland
I want it to erect an immortal tombstone

I'm as filthy as before: the spell I vomit
the blood I spit. A love that doesn't care for shame, a reckless interrogation

O, snow, this prophet, hypocrite, and traitor, an accomplice of evil
I want him to bare tombs where weeds can't grow

I take a fancy to its sole merit:
things I tell no one can spread beneath snow

Untitled

Can you come and sweep away my wilting: throw out dead flowers
cut withered leaves
But for now keep the lingering branches: keep the once fragrant path

—I hand you my twilight years, my wrinkled
heart
You can't blame me, we have walked through a lifetime for this meeting

There isn't much time, we must condense sleep
Repeat to me
the rivers, mountains, mornings and crowds you have passed

—the me you once loved falls again for you
then yawns
without grievance

Bright Full Moon,
Towering Tree Shadows

1

It was getting dark. A rooster crowed along the way, summoning a hen and chicks into the house. A dusk-soaked clutch of chicken strolled inside. Light was mild and tender on their feathers, the rooster's coxcomb a flashing red. How inspiring, their way of life, how uplifting.

The fowl entered by the back door, out from the setting sun, their bodies tinged with dry heat, and chirped around enjoyably. Once in the courtyard, some entered the chicken coop, while others made their way to a shelter in the southern corner.

It had been a while since the shelter was cleaned: a layer of chicken dung had accumulated on the ground, with mosquitoes buzzing around. The place was packed with sundries: a small wooden table, a large rectangular table, and a metallic stove for heating in winter. On the table and stove were a variety of things: packets of fertilizer, gourd scoops, discarded objects, and so on. Leaning against the western wall were a standing wooden bed with dull gray stripes, a bedside table, and some flimsy spider webs. Two ropes were suspended from a rafter and tied to a bamboo stick that was once used as a clothes rack, now buried under spider webs that swayed in the southern wind. Where was the spider? Might it be waiting for the old web to collapse before weaving another?

Just as it was getting dark, a brood of chickens entered, hesitant and cautious, as if someone were falling asleep in the house. After making dinner, Mother erected a net at the door, lest the chickens messed up the place when they woke up early the next morning. Someone had lived and died in this room. She was none other than my Grandma.

2

In the autumn of 2013, the fine weather lasted for days, and wild chrysanthemums were in full bloom outside the house. The sun shone bright, the courtyard was warm. I couldn't help but feel confident despite my filthy, fading life. When the sun could shine on anyone alive, one would naturally have a desire to live.

My aunt came by to visit Grandma. Now older, my aunt had surprisingly become gentler, and showed more care for Grandma. She would ask Grandma what she wanted to eat, even though Grandma wanted nothing but water. My aunt prepared her a glass of sugared water and asked if she needed anything else. Grandma said no, then lay down on the bed, her body to one side, and rested. My aunt stayed on a little and then left.

After a while, I went in to check on Grandma, who was still lying there as before. I figured that she must have been exhausted after mumbling to herself the whole night, so I didn't wake her up. She could have been dead by then. Even in her death, she chose not to let me know. After making lunch, I went in again: there she was, still in the same position. I touched her hand; it was cold. The sun at noon was piercing, and I blinked my eyes.

I rushed outside and called for my father, telling him that Grandma was dead. He responded, "I know. I'll come over right away." I yelled again, and he repeated, "I know. I'll come over right away." I then ran back to her room, and touched her hand, her face . . . As I realized she would never say a word again to me, my tears began to pour, as if it were already too late to grieve.

My parents did not send for someone to dress her up in burial clothes. Instead, they cleaned her body and did it themselves. Mother chanted, "Do be good, we'll dress you up nicely, so you won't be cold on the road . . ." As it was,

Grandma's body softened, as if ready to put on her burial clothes.

3

At sixty, Grandma had started to prepare her burial clothes. She was fastidious about details that would otherwise confuse me: the choice of material, the cotton undergarments, the size of her undergarments and coat, the specific number and placement of buttons, and so on. I had always thought of death as something remote, and never gave it a thought. No wonder Grandma blamed me for not being filial.

Grandma was just as fussy about clothes as celebrities are. Overjoyed with a new garment, she would say, *Oh, how fitting these clothes are, how superb the stitching.* Upon hearing her praise, we heaved a sigh of relief: *Surely these clothes will work out this time.* No sooner than a few days later, Grandma's clothes began to look weird: a sleeve longer by a centimeter or a finger, for instance, altered by Grandma herself, who, after all, had aged and could no longer sew properly. But as long as she felt comfortable in those clothes, it all seemed fine.

One year, I bought her a blouse that suffered the same fate. I was sad, so I never bought her clothes anymore. Not a piece of Grandma's clothing was authentic, in that she had modified them all beyond recognition. This threw my father in a rage, but it was futile. Any article of clothing that ended up in Grandma's possession was not to be worn, but altered.

This was why Grandma's burial clothes were altered numerous times, until she herself became confused, and couldn't remember anything about it. We laughed and told ourselves that perhaps it was better to have confused Grandma, who would then wear whatever clothes she was given.

By the time she wore whatever she was given, she had become too frail. No one would find her hiding in her room and altering clothes, like a child shrouded in guilt.

4

When one dies, the living burn paper money. I don't know why, but might it be a way to send off a soul? I had no idea if Grandma's soul was still in her room or if it had left by the main gate, since no one could feel her presence in the crowded funeral setting. My father had not anticipated the mounting responsibilities and tasks after Grandma's death, and was overwhelmed. I meant to call my brother but did not wish to disturb him in school. Were Grandma still alive, she would reprimand me, *Even Laozi's death wasn't a big deal, let alone mine?* Indeed, I took death so lightly, and did not think of informing anyone when she passed on.

After some time, I went ahead and sent a message to my brother: *Grandma has died.* I did not say *She has passed away,* or that *she has gone.* I plainly said *died.* Gone and back, back and then gone. Death was but a one-way street.

My brother drove back immediately and blamed me for not informing him beforehand; by the time he arrived, Grandma was already in her coffin.

The coffin was moved into the inner hall instead of the main hall. It was a sturdy coffin without paint. How frail and fragile Grandma's body was, like an infant in a box.

More people arrived, and soon death seeped into the crowd. Grandma's three sons were over sixty, seventy. They must have been too ashamed to weep. Grandma lived well into her nineties and had, over the years, unmasked death breath by breath before their eyes, reducing their sadness into nothingness.

Grandma also had a foster daughter. Both of them had been on intimate terms until recently. While Grandma converted to Christianity, my aunt was a devout Buddhist. Whenever she had to visit her daughter, Grandma would feign illness. Soon, they grew apart. When my aunt arrived, Grandma was placed in her coffin. My aunt touched the coffin and went around it, weeping dramatically yet without tears, so that I couldn't help but laugh.

To consult a Taoist priest on the date of her burial was the most important thing on our list of things to do. How unfortunate Grandma's life was: the priest came that same day but couldn't conduct the ritual between eleven at night and one in the morning. My father had to pay for a car service to transport Grandma's body for cremation. When she was alive, Grandma was most afraid of cremation, so imagine her defiance had she known of this.

At dusk, the coffin was reopened for us all to take a last look at Grandma: she appeared to be asleep, without a trace of worldly fatigue.

5

When my brother and I were in elementary school, Grandma was in her sixties, soon turning seventy. By then, she was a Christian. Christianity had just arrived in our village, and my parents became Christians because of my illness. Of course, I could never be cured of my disability, but my toothache disappeared, and ever since then, Grandma devoted herself to Christianity to the end of her life.

They did not read prayers from books. Instead, they relied on others to copy prayers on a notebook, paragraph by paragraph, under headings such as "Meals," "Sleep," "Chasing Ghosts," "Healing," etc. They seemed to perceive disease as separate from the experience of being haunted by a ghost. This struck me as a rather materialistic outlook, but in the end they were all touched by the Lord. We the young ones weren't fooled, but we couldn't help but feel awe before the cross.

Grandma was illiterate, so she needed others to help her with prayers. I woke up in the morning to do my homework with my brother while Grandma cooked. Once in a while, she would come in and ask us to teach her a sentence or two. Her memory was poor, so goodness knew how long it took us to teach her a prayer. But Grandma was fond of learning and welcomed every possible opportunity to recite prayers. This went on for years. Until my marriage, we shared a bed, so she would nag me at night for more prayers.

In those days, I found it a nuisance to teach Grandma about prayers. After working at them for some years, she managed to learn two books of prayer by heart. In her prime, she could even heal village children with her prayers. The vague power of her faith seemed so real.

6

Later, when her "supernatural powers" weakened, she stopped treating children with headaches. By then I had run out of patience to teach her prayers. She continued to pray before the cross day and night. At her age, kneeling was a challenge, getting up another, so she prayed while standing up. Perhaps after some time, she, too, became a little negligent and exhausted, and no longer bowed or prayed at meals.

No one knew when she became exasperatingly talkative: she would boast of her healing ability to anyone she met, how the Lord created miracles, how marvelous He was, and *Look, yet another nonbeliever who worships the devil . . .* She strongly opposed my mother's Buddhist practice and labeled it as "the evil cult." She added, "The Lord shined anew in my room last night." Indeed, the light of the Lord was white, the light of evil glaringly red. At first, we were intrigued by her stories, and grateful for the arrival of the Christ in our home. Later, after her endless reiterations, we no longer believed in her words. Grandma panicked: "Why would I lie at my age?"

Having exhausted all topics of conversation, she would recall her old times with pride glowing in her eyes. She spoke of how the Japanese invaded their village and captured young men. In fact, not all the invaders were Japanese; some were soldiers in disguise, and this was how Grandpa ended up being arrested. When Grandma learned of Grandpa's news back home, she took my father, then barely a year old, and left to look for my Grandpa. The villagers told her how ruthless the Japanese were and persuaded her not to.

But Grandma had made up her mind. She later told us, "I decided that if your Grandpa would not return, I'd die with him." She was so heroic then, and did what most women wouldn't—this became her glory and pride for the rest of her life.

Grandma continued, "I waited for him in a tent until it was late, and came across the chief. I wasn't afraid at all. I had no time for that. Your father was so obedient then. I told him to kowtow to the chief, and he did it right away. The chief was delighted, asked us a few questions, and freed your Grandpa." This was how my Grandma managed to save Grandpa, albeit in a muddled way. This became a familiar story at home.

Grandma narrated her past to us over and over, to the point that her heroism annoyed us and sounded unconvincing. I teased her, "Grandma salutes the Japanese, so she's a traitor!" This made Grandma jump. She ran after me, and yelled, "If I were a traitor, what about you and your father?" Grandma's legs were still strong then, so she could easily chase after me all over. I was so afraid of her catching up with me, yet I couldn't help laughing out loud.

7

Once the coffin was lifted onto the hearse, according to our custom, my father had to kneel before each pallbearer, but in our village we had our own rules: he should kneel and bow to everyone. But one of his knees was crooked, so it was heartbreaking to see him do so with his long mourning head-scarf draping down, as he seemed much smaller than his usual self.

Not many of us could make it to the crematorium. We waited at home, while she was now returned "earth to earth, ashes to ashes, dust to dust." I couldn't imagine her frail, tiny body being pushed into a furnace. Would her soul witness her own body and flesh being reduced into ash? Would she blame her children and grandchildren for not burying her as she had wished? Or would she just sigh, *I'm an old woman who will never bow down to anyone, so let my body burn, I'll feel no pain.*

Would she really feel no pain?

We waited for the others on the trail. The night was pitch-dark, but our voices mingled with one another, and our sorrows blurred. My father brought Grandma down from the car in a small urn. I didn't hold the urn, but I imagine it must have felt so light, like a child lying in my father's arms.

Even so, the urn was arranged to be placed in a coffin, like when one walks into a spacious, empty room and does not know where to stand. Grandma must have felt so apprehensive in this foreign place where no one came to her help when she yelled. Once the coffin was laid and buried, a person would disappear entirely from this world. Not a gust of wind. Darkness gathered around us and refused to dissipate. Grains of sand fell upon our hearts as we held our breath and couldn't weep.

8

When I was younger, Grandma frequently quarreled with Mother, but no matter what, Grandma's heart ached for my exhausted mother who never failed to make new clothes for Grandma each new year. Time and again, I wonder if they might feel lonely without each other's company. My mother never spared Grandma her sharp tongue and said mean things that would make Grandma "lose face," so they were at loggerheads. This was my worst childhood memory. After their quarrels, they would sleep over it for a few days before giving up their fight and return to being a close-knit family. Even as they aged, they never stopped fighting, just not as much as before.

Grandma hung a cross in her room. After converting to Buddhism, Mother placed an incense burner in the hall, where she burned incense on the first and fifteenth of each month. Grandma stubbornly believed that Buddhism was a cult and felt offended by Mother's practice. Once, she broke the incense burner. In turn, her own cross was torn off the wall. Still, Mother continued to burn incense, and Grandma persisted with her prayers. Both practiced their beliefs fervently.

One interesting incident: in order to test if the glue he bought worked effectively, my father glued a bowl on the altar. By chance, Grandma saw the bowl and wanted to take it away, but she couldn't move it. Taken by surprise, she was convinced that the hall was haunted. From that moment, she hurried in her steps when she had to pass by the hall, afraid of crossing paths with a ghost. We were amused for a long time, and laughed whenever we were reminded of this.

Another episode: my father bought packets of pesticides and hung them on the beam in front of the hall. Grandma saw them the moment she came in, and out of, the hall, and felt uncomfortable. She told me, "Look at your father: he buys pesticides and hangs them there for me to drink. Huh, I won't poison myself. I'll live to poke at your eyes." Again, we laughed our heads off a long time. But Grandma was old and couldn't remember anything after sleeping over it. When my father put away the pesticides, she, too, had forgotten what happened.

9

When Grandma was around, I found her vexing. She even wronged me every now and then. This ambitious old woman never revealed her vulnerabilities to anyone. No matter how intimate one was with her, she had to have the last word, even to the point of hurting herself. For a while, I was tired of her and thought her death would be a relief to us all. Now that she actually was dead, I could barely believe that she was gone for good.

After Grandma's passing, we lit her room for forty-nine days. The altar lamp burned day and night for Grandma to make her way to the underworld. Many a time, I went to her room, yelling, "Grandma, Grandma!" But once out of her room, I couldn't sense her presence. How chilling. Who could know how disappointed Grandma must have been in me, such that she had never once turned back.

As I sat in her room, I wondered how marvelous it might be were she still alive, even if it meant us fighting every day. Now that she was gone, the room empty, a void grew in my heart, never to be made whole again. I wanted to cry, but felt weak and sentimental.

If I told Grandma, *I'm on TV now, Grandma, and have been on TV many times,* she would look at me, her eyes squinting, *You, on TV? Can you even speak clearly?*

My Dog Is Called Little Wu

When I limp out the courtyard, she tags along
We pass a vegetable garden and ditch, going north to Grandma's

When I fall into the ditch, she wags her tail
I stretch my hand out, she licks the blood off my hand

Drunk, he claims he has a woman in Beijing
prettier than me. They go dancing when they run out of gas
He fancies dancing women
watches them shake their butts
He claims they know how to moan with pleasure: how lovely
    they sound, unlike me
not a word, my face covered

I eat in silence
throw meat to the dog, *Little Wu, Little Wu*
She wags her tail, yelps in joy
When he pulls my hair and knocks my head against the wall
Little Wu keeps wagging her tail
helpless before someone unafraid of pain

We walk behind Grandma's house
only to realize she has been dead for years

Ancestral Worship on
Tomb-Sweeping Day

After lunch, my parents visited Grandpa's tomb
I accompanied them to the crossroads and stopped
It had been years since I visited Grandpa, again I stopped midway

My parents shrank in the distance
Lanterns glittered in their hands: excellent sun
excellent rapeseed

The long-blossoming rapeseed's fragrance would fade
The usual spring sorrows felt hazy
—I had fallen in love with entrenched servitude

Chewing a flower
I saw some men working on a pylon
like stinging mosquitoes
who wouldn't fall with a thud
At this thought
firecrackers popped in a graveyard

Wheat Has Ripened

Wheat ripens first at my front door, next in Hengdian
and the Jianghan Plain

In moonlight meditation, wheat rubs against each other
All things on earth are in love now

In this vastness, how to find a grain of white
and inhabit it?

Late at night, I watch Father smoke with the moon on his back
—it constricts after harvesting thousands of hectares of wheat

O Father, your bliss is a brown wheat skin
Pain, a pure wheat heart

I am pleased to have landed here
like a sparrow skirting through the sky-blue

Early Winter Evening

Sunlight retreats from the backyard; it retreats so slowly
Pausing in between, like a choke of sobs
A northern breeze can't stir poplar leaves in the backyard
A jar of herbs mumbles on a stove in their depression: its odor rushes
out and hits an old sick body
She kneels in the courtyard, more coiled up than a leaf
A knife in her body coils up too
She tries to pull it out, slices off a piece of old love
This severe disease gets so inflamed in winter

Chinese medicine treats symptoms, not the disease
Yet she smells the scent of these herbs
Twelve in all: she picks Chinese angelica and nothing else
and dumps it into a pile of fallen leaves

Marriage

Why do I have a persimmon, why a persimmon

For years, someone plays tug-of-war in the marsh
A window facing north is shattered, someone suppresses the northern
    wind in her heart

What are you in this world, you can't speak clearly or walk steadily
You shitty woman, on what basis
won't you bow down to me

Mother, you never tell me why I have a persimmon
I ate a persimmon as a child, almost died because I was allergic

How I enjoy solitude: alone by a dusky river
washing wounds on my body
Things I can't do in this lifetime, I write them down in an epitaph
—let me leave, give me freedom

In the Cotton Fields

At noon, she straightens her back
Autumn wind slides down her back, the grass downhill a softer yellow
Tombs exposed, burnt paper money lingers since April

Already the third batch: crammed white lanterns hang in the air
Again she believes
these white dots have gathered to cheer up her days

She readjusts the tape on her hand
I've said, life pinched between five fingers
can't leak out

Carrying a bag of cotton on her way back, she falls
and gets up
Not one cloud in the sky
but many on the ground

Callosity

Bury you and your hands' calluses
But you must keep this callosity: the road to the underworld is interminably
    cold, so you can poke and play with it
If you turn back, I'll recognize you more easily

Papa, you know you're making things difficult for yourself
but you never say it out loud
Of life, disdain or respect, you never feel at ease speaking out

As someone's child, you might not have a choice
As your child, I dare not seek your compensation for my misery
I bury you with callused hands

As a strand of grass, I've often wished for you
a spring
not to praise your grandeur, but your peace
We won't see each other again, Papa, goodbye
Don't leave any sign along the way
Don't let this lifetime follow you

Love

In a sunny courtyard, a golden pitter-patter of sparrows
faded Chinese rose leaves look just fine

Time has an order. Life lays bare a bright side
its other side in need of love

I will run into the best landscape, the best folk
Wherever they are is my homeland
an ancestral temple where I hear stars in dialogue

Here I am, at this hour
The world shows me how landscapes undulate
However large its secret, however large the sky it opens

At this instant, struck by a secret
I weep, but keep my mouth shut

For You

At a plain teahouse, I like the you right before me, your plain gaze
Your beard, the look of last night's tossing and turning saddens me
Much of what I hope to offer you is lost on the way
save for pale spring colors outside the window

Since we met, you've never stopped loving others, one after another
I have no right to be jealous, but can only exile myself time and again
Living on to wait for your twilight years, to wait
for the crowd to disperse, the flame of your soul reduced to ash

I love you: I want to hug you
hug your worn-out worldly body
Because I love you
I forgive you for harming me, again and again, because of other women
I too have desires in my prime years, nights with a shattered body-mind
but never have I banished myself
I want my body as clean as my mind
even if not for the sake of seeing you

Autumn Rain

You walk past that street: lights now on
the rain hasn't stopped

It's been too long since we met. You are dripping wet from another world
I don't know where to start
wringing you dry

We praise the world, exhaust a lifetime
I praise you, but let this lifetime
sloppily drag on
Leaves fall on a straight path

Those who fail to catch the wind end up with hearts in knots
I thought a body that blocks wind
would leave you a line
of clear narrow sky
I still hope
to err over and over

Dusk on My Brow

1

I favor dusk, as if I were just as gentle and cool. Perhaps I should be embarrassed, describing myself as *gentle*, but I can't find a better and more calming word. We have man-handled so many words that I only dream of using them anew.

At this instant, the hour we call *dusk* has backed away, like a wave receding into its sea. Night is another wave that surges. I expand this space-time in my imagination, as if it were a snapped angel's trumpet full in bloom. I like its impotence and futility. Next to time, we are a never-ending failure, even if a moment such as this might turn out to be our consolation.

Here is an ambiguous boundary: barely a moment ago, a strand of twilight sparkled through a poplar, emanating an exquisite voice between its body and leaves. Night falls the next moment: I feel its gentleness as wind blows through the window. A windy hour is to me a gentle one.

2

AUGUST 26, 2015. 7:24 P.M.

As I type those words, the hour is past. Whereas certain details are invariably unfathomable, others aren't supposed to be fathomable. Time teaches us not to be greedy. It reveals eternity and simplicity via a moment of continuous flow.

My son will be attending school in two days. Right now, he is watching a movie on my bed. I hear noise and distorted voices from his computer. Our lamp glows slowly, slower than my son's growth. It feels like yesterday when we last played and fought with each other in the evening. In the twinkling of an eye, he is now a boy. The cruelty and grace of time is right within the same wave band.

Mother is gathering corn in our courtyard. She keeps coughing. Her cough is the abyss in this dusk. How I wish I could clog up the abyss, an act more exasperating than catching hold of time. We seem alive, yet death is at our feet, as if running into it whenever we trip and fall.

3

Evenings are best in August: we are blessed with this decades-old courtyard and its golden corn. Corn is the most erotic among all crops: its color, appearance, and taste fascinate me. Were I given a choice, I would like to be a grain of corn in this courtyard, soaked in this sun and twilight.

In our Jianghan Plain, corn is hardly considered a major crop. Rather, it leads a guerrilla's life. Wherever rice fails to grow, whenever a farmer feels like growing corn, we have corn. Gods have the last say in a harvest, but corn does not care for any of this: it grows as long as it finds land and light, and flourishes in wind and rain.

Every hour after the process of rooting is a good hour, each strand of light is ideal, each gust of wind makes it rejoice, each rain its gratitude. This is why it stretches out in the courtyard with such modesty, air, and pride. No one can be prouder than a cornstalk or calmer than a crop.

4

A kitten came to our house two months ago. Poor little thing, abandoned, and with dark fur as sharp as thorns. A black spot was stuck on its nose, as if painted by a naughty child. At first, the frail kitten could only moan an unbearably hoarse meow. It seemed out of breath. When Mother was released from the hospital, we prepared mudfish for our meals and ate meat. The kitten could thus feed on bones, and soon regained its strength. Now, it plays happily in its own chair and meows sweetly.

At lunch one day, I picked kernels of corn out of our pickles and threw them onto the ground. The kitten ate them up. Mother and I were surprised. I threw it peanuts, but it sniffed at them and walked away. Whenever Mother left kernels of corn on the floor, it would eat them all. What a strange cat. We have kept many cats, yet this is the first time I have seen a cat eating corn.

One afternoon, we were shucking corn when we caught sight of the kitten picking at corn in the courtyard. It was eating raw corn! Swaying its tiny head, it tried hard to chew on a raw kernel. How charming and naive. In the half-shadow of the roof, it kept on chewing. I asked Mother if it had eaten any mice. Mother said yes: one day, she killed a mouse and threw it to the cat; the cat pounced on it right away.

5

At sunset, worried about the coming rain, my father would gather up corn from the fields. Although we tend to rely on weather forecasts, forecasts can be as fickle as us humans. Trees are lush in August, when not a single leaf has fallen in our courtyard. Sheltered by its roof ridge, the space is void of shadows, too. A bamboo broom sweeps away gently. *Swish, swish*, like waves that testify to the presence of sea, just as the swishes of a broom sweeping away corn testify to the presence of my father and life.

A few days before drying our corn, we typically dry peanuts in the courtyard. Everything grows on our land, so we grow anything. Since my mother has fallen ill this year, my father is the only one taking care of the fields. He has been exhausted by days of harvesting peanuts: without rain to soak the soil, it is impossible for us to pull the peanuts out. So he has to use a spade to dig them out, one by one, for several days.

We dry peanuts and corn the same way. Corn is heavier, so it tumbles onto the ground with a duller sound. After dehydration, a crack emerges between a peanut and its shell. It is hard to describe the sound of their collision: it is the music of pride and contentment, humility and self-respect after harvesting. My father gathers them at dusk. A crop that hasn't witnessed at least a few dusks in this court-yard isn't considered the master's crop. I observe my father's hair, not yet white, and feel a little relieved about life.

6

When there is no work for me to do, I'd rather not stay indoors. A walk in the fields is most appealing to me. By the time I walk out the back door, dusk has fallen. But the setting sun is still a crescent—this is, to me, the best hour: whatever I need to do is now done, so with nothing else on my mind, I take a relaxing walk. If I am in a good mood, I will walk farther out, usually to the reservoir at the end of the village, go around it, and back. By then, the sky is dark, and dusk is over. But if I am in a bad mood, I will just hang around and watch dusk in its slow retreat.

The slowest to pull itself away is twilight on the grass, fickle and swaying in the wind. It falls aground inadvertently, and lingers awhile before vanishing without a trace. Light is nobler than water: when water vanishes, it leaves a stain, whereas light shrugs off a mess: it comes clean and goes strong, as if other things pale in its presence.

Twilight must have been intertwined with light, such that light seems most alluring at this instant: soft, tolerant, and considerate. It reminds me of the end-of-life rally before one dies. The phrase *end-of-life rally* sounds so heartbreaking, as if one exists in a bundle of light and puts up a last fight to shine for the last time, before one departs from the world.

I enjoy being in the evening fields, and among such exquisite shards of light. When light caresses my hair, I possess a day of bliss rising from my body and recasting itself upon it.

7

Dusk is regional. I fancy its regionalism. In my opinion, dusk feels more like Hengdian, and much like its dialect. One isn't bound merely by fate. One is destined on many other levels: for example, destined to walk in a certain place, or to hang around at such a time. The Hengdian dialect has a soft lilt, like the scent of a bitter gourd when cut. Dusk in Hengdian is just as soft.

One first hears the insects. Our land has gone to waste this year, so there are no crops, and bugs are breeding. I don't know how many they are, in comparison to previous years. At dusk, they stretch their wings and jump out, squeaking high and low, as if rejoicing in a new home. Yes, they have found their lost homeland, and I have found in them my childhood and hometown. The moon looks so clear, its breeze in ripples.

We are infatuated with exquisitely wild things: tiny animals, tiny voices, fine pride and sighs . . . and fine rays of light through short plants and on their bodies. When crops grow, I live in harmony with them; when there is no crop, I am in harmony with wild beasts and insects. I live in harmony with Hengdian because I am a part of my village.

8

Sometimes dusk seems to me an inner exile: when one is forced to leave home, home feels closer; a masked self is closer to truth. But I prefer to believe that one can never tell his or her truth. Truth once spoken tends to be false: we hear endless stories about suffering and beyond in life, stories with endless details but no end. This applies to me, and insects. Dusk falls on us, quietly, like infinite grief and joy.

I love how this hour reveals a world before my eyes: a realm of gentleness. Mountains let out a blue breeze, water moves in a paler blue, resisting in an immense fusion. I hear sharp whistles during such enchanting resistance. Although I can neither grasp nor speak of them, I indulge in these delusions.

You may walk far out into the field, but you can't walk past a strand of couch grass. Here you are, and there it is: it runs ahead of you wherever you go. Take a closer look, it is no more than what it is: rough edges, a protruding meridian, as if supported backstage by none other than our quiet earth.

This land is also my backstage, a place where I will rest in peace when I die.

9

I feel replenished right now, as the entirety of a day gradually flows, boosting a nobody like me with a sense of fulfillment. Time has its tangible flow; I am but a clean pond that waits for time to flow gently in me. Villagers back from the field look quite content, too: each day, each second glows in the field, subtle and still. How authentic, the arc of a body walking in the field at dusk.

As I write, I realize I have not said anything important about dusk. I can only immerse myself deeper in it. I am but a slice of it, and can't see it from a larger perspective. I am no more than a detail waiting for the whole picture. I praise dusk with my silence. My ode is a vestige of what it offers me and more.

Acknowledgments

Fiona Sze-Lorrain wishes to thank Diane Johnson, Christina Cook, Alessandra Bastagli, Donald Nicholson-Smith, James Allen, and the Columbia Institute for Ideas and Imagination in Paris.

ABOUT THE AUTHOR

Born in 1976 in Hengdian, a village in the county of Zhongxiang, Hubei Province, **Yu Xiuhua** is a poet from an impoverished rural background who suffers from cerebral palsy. Unable to attend college or find work, she was trapped in a small village and an arranged marriage. Yu began writing poetry in 1998. In 2014, her poem "Crossing Half of China to Fuck You" became an online sensation, launching her career as a celebrity poet and writer. Her poetry collection *Moonlight Rests on My Left Palm* (Guangxi Normal University Press, 2015) sold over three hundred thousand copies, a record for Chinese poetry titles of the past three decades. Yu received the Peasant Literature Award in 2016. *Still Tomorrow*, an award-winning documentary film about her life and poetry, was released to critical acclaim the same year. She was also the recipient of the Hubei Literary Prize in 2018. She lives in her native village Hengdian.

ABOUT THE TRANSLATOR

Fiona Sze-Lorrain is a poet, literary translator, editor, and zheng harpist who writes and translates in English, French, Chinese, and occasionally Spanish. The author of four poetry collections, most recently *Rain in Plural* (2020) and *The Ruined Elegance* (2016), both from Princeton University Press, she was a finalist for the 2016 Los Angeles Times Book Prize. She has also translated over a dozen books of contemporary Chinese, French, and American poetry, and was shortlisted for the 2020 Derek Walcott Prize for Poetry and the 2016 Best Translated Book Award. Named a 2019–20 Abigail R. Cohen Fellow at the Columbia Institute for Ideas and Imagination, she lives in Paris.

It takes a village to get from a manuscript to the printed book in your hands. The team at Astra House would like to thank everyone who helped to publish *Moonlight Rests on My Left Palm*.

EDITORIAL
Alessandra Bastagli
Olivia Dontsov

PUBLICITY
Rachael Small

MARKETING
Tiffany Gonzalez

SALES
Jack W. Perry

DESIGN
Jacket: Rodrigo Corral Studio
Interior: Richard Oriolo

PRODUCTION
Lisa Taylor
Alisa Trager
Rebecca Baumann

COPYEDITING & PROOFREADING
Janine Barlow
Nancy Seitz

COMPOSITION
Westchester Publishing Services

Λ

ABOUT ASTRA HOUSE

Astra House is dedicated to publishing authors across genres and from around the world. We value works that are authentic, ask new questions, present counter-narratives and original thinking, challenge our assumptions, and broaden and deepen our understanding of the world. Our mission is to advocate for authors who experience their subject deeply and personally, and who have a strong point of view; writers who represent multifaceted expressions of intellectual thought and personal experience, and who can introduce readers to new perspectives about their everyday lives as well as the lives of others.